EDGERTON PARTY ROUTE TO MONTANA 1863

SOUTH DAKOTA

FORT LARAMIE

SCOTT'S BLUFF

COLUMBUS

OMAHA

CHIMNEY ROCK

NORTH PLATTE RIVER

FORT KEARNY

NEBRASKA
KANSAS

December 1977

Norma and Wendell Maney

From Montana Historical Society

A Governor's Wife on the Mining Frontier

Number Seven of the Series

UTAH, THE MORMONS, AND THE WEST

The purpose of this series is
to make available both unpublished manuscripts
and others that are now out of print.
Selection is based upon
their intellectual appeal as accurate history
and their emotional interest
as good literature.

Mary Wright Edgerton

A Governor's Wife on the Mining Frontier

THE LETTERS OF MARY EDGERTON
FROM MONTANA, 1863–1865

Edited and with an Introduction by

James L. Thane, Jr.

Published by Tanner Trust Fund
University of Utah Library
Salt Lake City, Utah

For Merna

Acknowledgments

I am indebted to many people who have assisted in the preparation of this study including Mrs. Harriet Meloy, librarian of the Montana Historical Society, who first alerted me to Mrs. Edgerton's letters. She and the Society's archivist, Brian Cockhill, cheerfully provided much-needed help and made my visits to Helena both profitable and enjoyable. Portions of this manuscript originally appeared in *Montana, the Magazine of Western History*, and the magazine's editor, Mrs. Vivian Paladin, has generously allowed me to republish them here. All photographs used in this book are provided by the Montana Historical Society.

I am especially grateful to Dr. Malcolm J. Rohrbough who read the manuscript several times and made valuable suggestions for its improvement. My principal obligation is expressed in the dedication.

November, 1975
Moline, Illinois   J.L.T.

Contents

Illustrations

Introduction

$\mathcal{O}$N JUNE 1, 1863, a thirty-six-year-old woman from Tallmadge,
Ohio, left her home, her family, and her friends, and set out to
follow her husband in the pursuit of his political ambitions. Twice
before those ambitions had taken her from Tallmadge to Washington, D.C., but now, in the early summer of 1863, they were
leading her twenty-five hundred miles away to the goldfields of
Idaho, on the very edge of American civilization.

The woman was Mary Wright Edgerton. Her husband,
Sidney, had twice been elected to Congress, and in 1863, as Edgerton finished his second term, President Abraham Lincoln had
appointed him chief justice of the newly created Idaho Territory.
Mr. Edgerton was decidedly more enthused about the move to
Idaho than was his wife. As their eldest daughter later recalled,
"I know how bitter for her was the thought of leaving her twin
sister and her home." Mr. Edgerton, however, "welcomed the
opportunity to aid in the building of a new Territory, without
concerning himself about the womenfolks' homesickness or the
risks we must run to get there." [1]

The trip to Idaho took them from Tallmadge to Omaha, by
way of Cleveland, Detroit, Chicago, and St. Joseph. They then
traveled across the plains through present-day Nebraska, Wyoming, and Idaho into what is now southwestern Montana to the
small mining camp of Bannack.

The experience was not an enviable one. The trip across the
plains, though not as dangerous as contemporary western fiction
has portrayed it, was nonetheless long, uncomfortable, and difficult. And things did not improve much when the family settled in

[1] Martha Edgerton Plassman, "Judge Edgerton's Daughter," typescript
(Montana Historical Society, Helena), 66.

1

Bannack, a crudely constructed mining camp on the eastern side of the Rocky Mountains. Mrs. Edgerton, who had spent much of her life in a large house and whose family had seldom been without domestic help, now found herself confined to a small log cabin with a leaky dirt roof and inadequate heating facilities. Domestic help was virtually nonexistent, and thus all of the housework now fell to her and the members of her family. In Tallmadge, she had enjoyed the company of a circle of relatives and friends, but she found few respectable women in Bannack. It was, almost exclusively, a town made up of men who had come alone to the gold-fields, intent on making their fortunes and then escaping back to civilization in "the States."

To make matters worse, Mr. Edgerton was gone a good part of the time. In January, 1864, he left the territory for several months and returned to Washington, D.C., to lobby for the dividing of the Idaho Territory. He left his wife, then pregnant, alone, with only their thirteen-year-old daughter, an unfamiliar doctor, and Edgerton's niece Lucia Darling to help her through the pregnancy and all that it involved. In July, when Edgerton did finally return, he arrived as governor of the new Montana Territory. Mary Edgerton was now Montana's first lady, but the distinction did not mean very much, for her husband's promotion to the governorship did little to change their lifestyle.

During her three-and-a-half months on the plains and two years in Bannack, Mrs. Edgerton wrote a series of letters to her family in Ohio, vividly describing her journey over the plains and her life on the frontier. She wrote almost all of her letters to her twin sister, Mrs. Martha Carter, though she also corresponded with her mother and with another sister, Mrs. Lucy Ann Shaw. She attempted to write at least one letter a week to someone at home, and although directed primarily to her sister, she intended that the letters be circulated among all her various relatives. She strove to be faithful to this intention, and letters survive for slightly more than half of the weeks that the Edgertons were in Bannack. Generally, she started her letters on Sundays and finished them through the week as she had time, often concluding a letter in haste so that it could go out in a mail that was just about to leave. In return, she expected that the family back in Tallmadge would write to her at least once a week and she was bitterly disappointed when they did not or when, for one reason or another, the mails were delayed.

Her relatives saved many of her letters, and years later, one of her younger daughters found them scattered all over the floor of the attic in the old family home in Akron. The daughter, Nina Whitman, collected the letters and shortly before her death, gave them to her niece, Mrs. Harold Archibald, one of Mrs. Edgerton's granddaughters. Mrs. Archibald in turn donated them to the Montana Historical Society in 1962, and they are now the property of the Society.

Mary Edgerton was a witness to many of the important developments in Montana's early history, and her letters home provide additional information about those events. But much more important than that, they furnish a fresh and intriguing insight into a lady's life on the mining frontier. The letters are significant not only to Montana history but to the history of the frontier in general, for in many ways, Bannack was typical of scores of western mining camps, and Mary Edgerton had much in common with the women who inhabited them. The literature of western history contains many memoirs, journals, diaries, and letters of explorers, gold miners, ranchers, merchants, and the like — almost all of them men. There are fewer such records to document the lives of the women who also served. The letters of Mary Edgerton provide such a view and thus constitute a valuable primary source for a better understanding of life on the American frontier.

Mary Edgerton was born in Tallmadge on January 21, 1827, the daughter of Alpha and Lucy Foster Wright. Her mother was a native of New Hampshire, her father the son of a revolutionary war veteran from Connecticut who had settled in Ohio's Western Reserve near the turn of the nineteenth century. Mr. and Mrs. Wright had twelve children, eleven of whom survived to adulthood. Of these, Mrs. Edgerton was closest to her twin sister Martha and named her eldest child for her.

Tallmadge was a small community, five miles from Akron in northeastern Ohio. Almost all of its residents were descendents of New England emigrants and the town retained a strong New England flavor. The village was patterned after the plan of many New England towns, built around a town square where the town hall and the local church were located. Almost all of the residents were either Congregationalists or Presbyterians, and the Wrights belonged to the local Congregational church. Education was important to the people in the community, and the town hall contained an academy for the town's more advanced students. Some of the area farmers sent their sons away to college, principally to Yale and to Western Reserve College.[2]

Alpha Wright farmed about one hundred acres a mile south of Tallmadge, and apparently prospered at it. By 1850, his family lived in a large two-story frame house with thirteen or fourteen rooms, an attic, a large cellar, and an orchard in the yard.[3] He was an avid reader and stressed the importance of education both for his sons and his daughters. William Wright, one of Mary's elder brothers, was a founder of Oberlin College in Oberlin, Ohio. The future Mrs. Edgerton attended Oberlin for a time and later taught school as had her mother before her.[4]

Sometime in the 1840s, Mary Wright met her husband-to-be, Sidney Edgerton, a law student who moved to Akron in 1844. Edgerton, a native of New York, was also a descendent of New England lineage, the son of Amos and Zerviah Graham Edgerton. He was born August 17, 1818, in Cazenovia, New York, and grew up in that state. For a time he taught school, and in 1844 he arrived in Akron and became the student of a prominent Akron attorney, Rufus Spaulding. To support himself, he taught for a time at the Tallmadge Academy. In 1845 he entered the Cincinnati Law School and graduated in 1846. He opened his practice in Akron and became increasingly interested in politics and in the

2 Ibid., 1–6.

3 Ibid., 13–15.

4 Martha Edgerton Plassman, "How It Chanced," typescript (MHS).

crusade against slavery. In 1848, he was a delegate to the Buffalo, New York, convention that created the Free-Soil party.[5]

At some point during this period, Edgerton began his courtship of Mary Wright. Her parents originally opposed the match because Edgerton was "without the pale of the church." [6] Finally, however, her parents relented, and the two were married in Tallmadge on May 18, 1849. For a time they lived in Tallmadge, and their first child, Martha, was born in the home of Mrs. Edgerton's parents on May 14, 1850. Shortly thereafter, the family moved to Akron where Edgerton continued his law practice and his interest in politics. In 1852, he was elected prosecuting attorney for Summit County, Ohio, on the Free-Soil ticket, and in 1856 he was a delegate to the first Republican national convention.

After six years in Akron, the family moved back to Tallmadge and Edgerton purchased his father-in-law's farm. For a time he managed the farm and commuted daily the five miles to his law practice in Akron. In 1858, he was elected to Congress for the first time, running as a Republican, anti-slavery candidate in an area that strongly opposed the "peculiar institution." He then sold the farm and the family moved into a house in Tallmadge owned by Mrs. Edgerton's mother. The Edgerton children lived with Mrs. Wright while their mother accompanied Edgerton to Washington when Congress was in session.[7]

Edgerton was reelected in 1860, but encountered difficulty in 1862. Ohio's congressional delegation was reduced from twenty-one to nineteen in that year, and Edgerton's district, the Eighteenth, was reorganized. Portage and Stark counties were severed from the district, while Lake and Cuyahoga counties, which included Cleveland, were added to Summit County, Edgerton's home, to make up the new Eighteenth District. Edgerton sought

[5] Wilbur F. Sanders, "Notes on Montana History" (Hubert H. Bancroft Collection, Bancroft Library, Berkeley, California) ; Martha Edgerton Plassman, "Biographical Sketch of Hon. Sidney Edgerton, First Territorial Governor," *Contributions to the Historical Society of Montana*, III (1900), 331–34; Paul C. Phillips, "Sidney Edgerton," *Dictionary of American Biography*, VI, 20.

[6] Plassman, "Judge Edgerton's Daughter," 10.

[7] Martha Edgerton Plassman, "A Reminiscence of 1866," typescript (MHS) ; Plassman, "Judge Edgerton's Daughter," 47.

Sidney Edgerton

nomination for a third term, and the *Summit County Beacon* supported him. But in the convention Summit County had only forty-one votes, Lake County had twenty-seven, and Cuyahoga County had eighty-one. On September 26, the paper noted that the convention had given the nomination to Edgerton's old law mentor, Rufus Spaulding of Cleveland. Since Spauling had formerly been a resident of Summit County he drew support from both Summit and Cuyahoga delegates. Spaulding went on to win Edgerton's old seat in the general election.[8]

[8] See the *Summit County Beacon* (Akron, Ohio), August 21, September 5, September 26, October 2, and October 30, 1862.

As a reward for his loyal service to the Republican party, Edgerton was appointed chief justice for the Idaho Territory that Congress had created in March, 1863. By then the Edgerton family included four children: Martha (Mattie), born in 1850; Wright, born November 14, 1853; Sidney, born June 6, 1856; and Pauline, born July 11, 1858. At least one child, a boy named Franklin, had died in infancy and was buried in Tallmadge. In addition, Lucia Darling, Edgerton's niece, lived with the family.

Mrs. Edgerton's view of her husband's appointment to the Idaho bench can only be surmised. Probably she was not consulted in the matter, and if she had any objections, she no doubt kept them to herself. It is clear that she was deeply attached to Tallmadge and to her friends and numerous relatives there. It is also apparent that her absence from them pained her greatly. Still, she was "a woman whose own wishes were always subordinate to those of her family." [9] Accordingly, she tried to put the best possible face on the situation as she prepared herself and her family for the long trek across the plains and for what would ultimately prove to be two years in the wilderness of the Far West.

THE FRIENDS AND RELATIVES OF MARY EDGERTON

In her letters home, Mrs. Edgerton makes frequent reference to her friends and to members of her family. Where possible these individuals have been identified:

Abbie and William — Abbie and William Chandler of Parma, Michigan. Abbie Chandler was probably Mrs. Edgerton's sister.

Alla — Alla Carter, Mrs. Edgerton's niece. She was the daughter of Mrs. Edgerton's sister, Martha Carter.

Almarette — Almarette Geer, a young girl hired by Mrs. Sanders to help her with her children on the trip across the plains.

Ben (Benja.) — Benjamin Wright, Mrs. Edgerton's brother.

[9] Plassman, "Judge Edgerton's Daughter," 63.

Mr. Booth — A member of the Edgerton party on the trip across the plains.

Mr. Carter — Homer Carter, a Tallmadge merchant married to Mrs. Edgerton's sister Martha.

Charlie and Richard — Charlie Sackett and Richard Fenn, friends from Ohio who came to Montana in mid-1864.

Mr. Chipman — A member of the Edgerton party on the trip across the plains.

Clem — Clement Wright, Mrs. Edgerton's brother.

Edgerton, Volney — Sidney Edgerton's brother.

Franky — Frank Edgerton, Mrs. Edgerton's son who died in infancy in Ohio.

Franny — Franny Carter, Mrs. Edgerton's niece. She was the daughter of Mrs. Edgerton's sister, Martha Carter.

Mr. Gridley — Leonard Gridley, a member of the Edgerton party on the trip across the plains.

Hattie — Harriet Sanders, wife of Edgerton's nephew, Wilbur F. Sanders.

Henry — Henry Tilden, Edgerton's nephew who traveled with the family to Bannack.

Homer — Homer Carter, Mrs. Edgerton's nephew. He was the son of Mrs. Edgerton's sister, Martha Carter.

Howard — Howard Carter, Mrs. Edgerton's nephew. He was the son of Mrs. Edgerton's sister, Martha Carter.

Julia and Mr. Breeman — Julia Breeman was possibly another of Mrs. Edgerton's sisters.

Lucia — Lucia Darling, Edgerton's niece who accompanied the family to Montana.

Lucy — Lucy Wright, wife of Mrs. Edgerton's brother Clem.

Lucy Ann — Lucy Ann Shaw, Mrs. Edgerton's sister.

Martha — Mrs. Martha Carter, Mrs. Edgerton's twin sister.

Mary — Mary Carter, Mrs. Edgerton's niece. She was the daughter of Mrs. Edgerton's sister, Martha Carter.

Mattie — Martha Edgerton, Mrs. Edgerton's eldest daughter.

Nellie — Nellie Wright, wife of Mrs. Edgerton's brother Benjamin.

Pauline — Pauline Edgerton, Mrs. Edgerton's second daughter.

Sanders, Junius — Brother of Wilbur F. Sanders.

Mr. Shaw — Mrs. Edgerton's brother-in-law, married to her sister Lucy Ann.

Sidney — Sidney Edgerton, Mrs. Edgerton's second son.

Thomas, Mary — A girl who worked as a domestic for Mrs. Edgerton in Tallmadge.

Mr. Thompson — Francis Thompson, a close friend of the Edgerton family in Bannack.

Upson, James — A brother-in-law of Harriet Sanders.

Wilbur — Wilbur F. Sanders, Edgerton's nephew.

Wright — Wright Edgerton, Mrs. Edgerton's eldest son.

Chapter 1

Across the Plains to Bannack

TWO PRINCIPAL ROUTES were open to Idaho in 1863. The first involved an ocean voyage either around Cape Horn or across the Panamanian Isthmus, up the Pacific Coast to Oregon, then up the Columbia and Snake rivers to Lewiston on the western border of Idaho. The Edgertons rejected this route because of the danger of malaria in Panama or the possibility of shipwreck around the Horn. Most important, Mrs. Edgerton "had an uncontrollable fear of being on water." [1]

The second route was overland by rail from Ohio to St. Joseph, Missouri, then upriver to Omaha, and by wagon from Omaha to Idaho. Mrs. Edgerton's brother, Benjamin Wright, had gone overland to California with a group of gold seekers and urged the party to take the overland route. This advice, coupled with their reservations about the ocean voyage, convinced the Edgertons to go overland.

They left Tallmadge early on a Monday morning, June 1, 1863. The party included Mr. and Mrs. Edgerton; their children (Mattie, thirteen; Wright, ten; Sidney, seven; and Pauline, five); Sidney Edgerton's niece Lucia Darling, twenty-three; and his nephew Henry Tilden, a teenager. Lucia Darling was the daughter of Edgerton's sister Pauline. Pauline was "considerably older"

[1] Plassman, "Judge Edgerton's Daughter," 63.

11

than Sidney, and apparently she and her husband had assumed some of the responsibility of raising him after the death of Edgerton's father. Pauline died in 1850, and the circle was completed when her ten-year-old daughter went to live with the Edgertons in Tallmadge. Before the move to Idaho, Miss Darling taught school for several years in Ohio, all the time living with the Edgertons.[2] Henry Tilden reportedly had contracted tuberculosis in Ohio, and his parents sent him west with the Edgertons in the hope that the move to Idaho would improve his health.[3]

The party also included another of Edgerton's nephews Wilbur F. Sanders, who would later become prominent in Montana politics; his wife Harriet (Hattie); and their children, James, age four and Willie, age two. Mrs. Sanders employed a young woman Almarette Geer to help with her children. The group took carriages to Cuyahoga Falls, about three miles from Tallmadge, and then took the train to Cleveland. In Cleveland, two men, a businessman named Leonard Gridley and a Mr. Booth, joined the party. Booth had crossed the plains once before, and consequently, he became the party's "guide."

From Cleveland, the Edgerton party took a boat across Lake Erie to Detroit. The crossing was rough and some of them became seasick. From Detroit they took the train by way of Chicago to the western terminus of the railroad at St. Joseph. From there, they moved up the Missouri on a steamboat. They traveled only by day and tied up at night. Consequently, the trip took two days and nights.

On arriving in Omaha, the group checked into the Herndon Hotel and began preparations for the trip across the plains. Omaha in 1863 was a beehive of activity, the jumping-off point for hundreds of people crossing the plains to the Far West. There emigrants purchased the wagons, teams, and supplies essential to the overland journey, and there they said goodbye to civilization. One

[2] Undated letter from an unidentified granddaughter of Sidney Edgerton (Lucia Darling Collection, MHS); see also, *Warren* [Ohio] *Daily Tribune*, August 18, 1905, and Ruth Nichol, "Lucia Aurora Darling, Pioneer Teacher," *Delta Kappa Gamma Bulletin* (June, 1943).

[3] Jack Toole, "The Founding of Bannack, Montana," typescript (MHS).

Wilbur F. (nephew of Sidney Edgerton) and Harriet (Hattie) Sanders

emigrant, passing through the city a year after the Edgertons, noted that in the business district were "stores and warehouses combined, where goods were brought up from the warves and reloaded into great freight wagons to supply the posts and isolated points out on the trails or sold across the counter to a shifting crowd of emigrants, indians, and local residents." In addition, there were a number of saloons and dance halls where citizens and emigrants "were being relieved of their surplus cash through the agency of velvet-handed card experts or the age-old trinity, wine, women and song." [4]

[4] Arthur J. Dickson, ed., *Covered Wagon Days: A Journey Across the Plains in the Sixties, and Pioneer Days in the Northwest; from the Private Journals of Albert Jerome Dickson* (Cleveland, 1929), 51–52.

The men of the Edgerton party took several days to purchase wagons, oxen, and essential supplies. Into the latter category fell rifles and pistols as well as a few cows to provide milk for the children, a pony for the children to ride, and a dog which they hoped would be of service both for hunting and as a watch dog. The dog turned out to be something of a disappointment, and Mattie Edgerton concluded that it was "absolutely good for nothing." [5]

They purchased four wagons, each with two yoke of oxen and two cows. They chose oxen to pull the wagons because of their reputation for being hardy work animals, and because they had been told that the oxen would be much less attractive to the Indians than horses. The principal foodstuffs they took with them included bacon, ham, coffee, tea, salt, sugar, some dried fruit, and canned peaches. Some of these supplies the women had carefully packed and brought with them from Ohio; the remainder they purchased in Omaha.

Upon their arrival in Omaha, the group was surprised to learn that James Upson, Mrs. Sanders's brother-in-law, was on his way to Omaha. Some of the party feared that he would try to talk Mrs. Sanders out of making the journey. Upon his arrival, Upson did try to persuade Mrs. Sanders and her two small children to remain at home because her widowed mother feared for their safety on the plains. His plea was in vain, however, and Mrs. Sanders refused to stay behind.

While in Omaha, the Edgerton women met a number of other ladies who had been over the plains, and these women advised them that the trip would be particularly hard on their complexions. Consequently, to protect themselves from the sun, wind, and rain, the women in the party procured oil-silk masks. These consisted of semi-circular pieces of silk with holes cut for the eyes and nose. The Omaha women also advised them to cover their canteens with flannel to keep the water cold, and alarmed the younger girls by telling them stories of Indian atrocities on the plains. However, the men of the company were apparently little

[5] The Edgertons' stay in Omaha is described in Mary Edgerton's letter to her sister, June 10, 1863, and in Plassman, "Judge Edgerton's Daughter," 73–77.

concerned about the danger from Indians, even though, with the exception of Sanders who had seen some service in the Union Army, they were "almost as unskilled as the women in the use of firearms." [6] According to his daughter, Edgerton had an "unlimited faith in Indian chivalry, gained from the reading of Cooper's novels. . . . He felt sure Indians would not attack a train carrying women and children." [7]

While in Omaha, Mrs. Edgerton availed herself of the opportunity to write her first letter home, bringing her relatives up to date on the progress of the trip: [8]

Omaha, Neb.
June 10th, 1863

Dear Sister,

We have had three rainy days since we arrived here, but the sun is shining this morning, so I think the storm is over. Our Landlord says that it always storms three days at least. We have had a very pleasant journey so far with the exception of crossing the lake. The children have all stood the journey "remarkably" well. Hattie says that her children have not made half the trouble since she started with them that they used to make her at home. We are all well. We were all very much surprised to hear that James Upson was at St. Joseph waiting for a boat to come up here; he telegraphed yesterday to Wilbur. We can't imagine what he is coming for. I am terribly afraid that he is coming for Hattie but I hope not; he will not get here before tomorrow night.

[6] Plassman, "Judge Edgerton's Daughter," 74.

[7] Ibid.

[8] In editing Mrs. Edgerton's letters, I have made only those changes in spelling and punctuation that were necessary for reasons of clarity. Principally, these changes involve capitalization and inserting periods. Often, Mrs. Edgerton began sentences without using capital letters, and occasionally she neglected to put periods at the end of her sentences. In such cases I have substituted capitals for lowercase letters and have inserted periods. Occasionally she abbreviated words, and in some instances I have written them out in full. In addition, in each of her letters, Mrs. Edgerton inquired about the health and activities of her family and friends in Ohio. In a few instances I have left these questions in the text of the letters to indicate Mrs. Edgerton's concern for "all the folks at home," but in most cases I have deleted them. In no instance has the meaning of the letters been altered by these changes.

Mrs. Edgerton wrote primarily to her twin sister Martha, but occasionally she wrote to her other sisters as well. Unfortunately, most of the envelopes for the letters in this collection were sold separately to a stamp collector and it is often impossible to determine to which of her sisters Mrs. Edgerton was writing.

I wish you could have come as far as this place with us; you would have enjoyed it so much. The country from Quincy to St. Jo. is perfectly beautiful. I never saw anything begin to equal it. The railroad passes through rolling prairies and many of them were covered as far as we could see with beautiful flowers. I kept wishing that you were along with us, you would have enjoyed it so much. We were on the river two days and nights. We all enjoyed it very much. The boat was new and everything was neat and clean and our <u>living</u> was of the very best. We had everything on the table that anyone could wish, even to green peas and straw-berries. Wild strawberries are ripe here. Garden strawberries were ripe some time ago, everything is earlier here than in Ohio. I think it strange for it is farther north here than there.

Mr. Edgerton rec'd a few lines from Mr. Carter[9] yesterday and will answer it soon. He has bought wagons and is going out this afternoon to look at oxen. We expect to have one yoke of cows to every team. I hardly think we shall be able to start from here before next Monday. Our goods all got here yesterday.

We have formed some very pleasant acquaintances here. There are a number of ladies here that have been over the plains. We are going out this afternoon to see some of them to find out what we shall most need on our journey. I would like to [know] how you all are this morning and know what you were doing. . . . It is a pity that we did not bring Blackie with us to take over the plains for cats sell at ten dollars apiece. We might make a small fortune if we could take enough cats with us. Don't wonder at the poor writing or mistakes for I am writing in the parlor where there are at least a dozen talking. Mattie wrote a letter to Mary when she was on the boat but it is written so poorly that she don't want to send it. . . .

I hope we shall hear from you all soon. Love from all to all.

Mary

In Omaha, a druggist named Chipman joined the Idaho-bound party, and thus upon departing that city, the group con-sisted of sixteen members: six men, three women, and seven chil-dren. They left Omaha on the evening of June 16, in a large carriage, joined their teams, and traveled two-and-a-half miles before stopping to spend their first night on the plains. They awoke the following morning to discover that one yoke of oxen had dis-appeared during the night. The men spent nearly all day looking

---

[9] Homer Carter, a Tallmadge merchant, was Mrs. Edgerton's brother-in-law.

for the animals while the women rearranged the supplies they had packed in the wagons. They did not find the oxen until late in the afternoon and consequently did not begin their second day's journey until 5:00 p.m. They had "a pleasant ride of three miles and camped near a creek." [10]

That night they were hit by the first thunderstorm of their trip. It rained very hard, but did no damage and the party got an early start the morning of June 18. At first they experienced some difficulty controlling their teams. The oxen were young and only partially broken, and the men of the party had had no experience in driving them. Consequently, they hired a teamster who accompanied them for about a week, teaching the men how to handle the oxen.

Once out onto the plains, the company settled into a fairly regular routine. Their route out of Omaha took them over a trail variously called the Overland Trail, the Oregon Trail, or the Mormon Road. In the beginning, it ran through the valley of the Platte River in central Nebraska, along the north bank of the river. Usually, the group rose early, breakfasted, and then began the day's travel. They moved very slowly, stopping an hour for the noon meal, and halting in time to do chores such as milking cows, gathering fuel, and putting up their single tent, before darkness overtook them. Consequently, they averaged only about ten miles a day. The Edgertons and their smaller children slept in the tent and the others slept either in or under the wagons.

Everyone had his or her specific duties around the camp. The women had charge of the younger children, did dishes, washed clothes, and other routine chores. Lucia Darling did much of the cooking on a small sheet iron camp stove. The men in turn drove the teams, cared for the animals, stood guard duty, and hunted for game. Since their progress was so slow, members of the train often

[10] Harriet P. Sanders, "Diary of a Journey from Omaha to East Bannack City in the Summer of 1863 via Kearny, Laramie, South Pass, and Lower Snake Ferry," June 17, 1863. Both Mrs. Sanders and Miss Darling kept detailed diaries of the trip over the plains. Edgerton's daughter Martha later wrote several reminiscences of the trip and discussed it at length in her autobiography, "Judge Edgerton's Daughter." All three accounts are in the Montana Historical Society Archives, and, together with the surviving letters of Mary Edgerton, they provide a very complete account of the trip.

walked ahead of the wagons, sometimes picking flowers or collect-
ing stones. The women sometimes walked far enough ahead of the
wagons to stop under a tree and write letters or entries in their
diaries while waiting for the train to catch up with them. The children played with what few toys they had brought with them or
made up games as they went along. Mr. Edgerton brought a few
books and occasionally read aloud as the wagons rolled along. The
men did not drive the teams from seats on the wagons, but rather
walked along side of the oxen, barking commands and using their
whips to keep the animals on the road.

From time to time, the party encountered other wagon trains
of varying size and sometimes traveled with them for part of the
way, but most of the time the train remained small. Generally, the
party observed Sunday as a day of rest, and did not travel unless
they felt it imperative to do so. On Sundays they often slept late
and then spent the day reading, writing letters, or simply relaxing.

For the most part, the trip was fairly routine, but occasionally
the monotony was broken by the rumors of nearby Indians, by a
visit to an interesting landmark, or by the necessity of crossing a
river. The river crossings proved to be potentially the most dangerous part of the trip. On June 23, for example, they were forced
to cross the Loup River near Columbus, Nebraska, some sixty miles
west of Omaha. The Loup is a sluggish river, but its shifting, sandy
bottom made it difficult to ford. Fortunately, a rope ferry was in
operation to take the wagons part of the way across. They were
then landed on a sand bar in midstream from which they forded
the rest of the way by themselves.[11] The Sanders wagon went
across first, and "had a great deal of trouble. . . . The cattle went
nicely for a short distance and then stopped stone still notwith-
standing the urging and lash of the driver." The wagons were
marooned in midriver until two other yoke of oxen were brought
to pull them out.[12]

That same day, the party encountered the first sign of possible
Indian problems. They received word that on the previous day a
group of Pawnee Indians had engaged in a skirmish with some

[11] See Dickson, *Covered Wagon Days*, 54–57.
[12] Sanders Diary, June 23, 1863.

Sioux only fifteen miles from the Edgerton campground. For safety's sake, they camped near a company of government troops taking provisions to Fort Laramie, and Mrs. Sanders noted that the men kept their guns loaded and were "ready for a brush." The night passed without incident, however, and in the morning they awoke "all safe and sound." [13] After this they generally posted a guard during the night, but had no difficulty at all with the Indians.

On June 25, the train stopped for lunch at Lone Tree Station, about 115 miles from Omaha, and Mrs. Edgerton wrote a letter to her sister:

Lone Tree Station
June 25, 1863

Dear Sister,

I have a few minutes to write this noon while we are waiting for the cattle [which] are eating.

I wish you could have seen where we camped last night. We camped in the middle of a large prairie that was completely covered with the sensitive plant in blossom. You can't imagine how beautifully it looked. I have gathered a quantity of the seed and will send you some. I hope you will succeed in making it grow. Night before last I did not sleep much for we were within a few miles of where the Pawnees and Sioux had had a fight the day before and we did not know but they might attack us. We camped near a government train and shall keep near them until they get to Fort Laramie. The people around here think that there is no danger of their attacking the whites as long as they are fighting among themselves but we thought it best to guard ourselves as well as we could. We are going farther from them every day. We have had beautiful weather to travel so far — have had but one shower and that was on the second night after we left Omaha, and that was such a shower. It was a terrific thunder shower. I never saw such lightening or heard such thunder.

3 o'clock P.M. We have just met one company of soldiers coming from Fort Kearney to assist the Pawnees. The Capt. has gone on to see if he can get them to come to some settlement. We are now about one hundred and thirty miles from Omaha, in the Platte Valley. We are in the sight of the river now all the time and most of the road we have been over this week has been right on the banks of the river. It is a wide river but very shallow. A man can wade across it almost anywhere.

[13] Ibid., June 23 and 24, 1863; Darling Diary, June 23 and 24, 1863.

We are almost to a post office so I will not stop to finish this but [will] send it as it is. I would like to write more if I had time. Goodbye. Love to all.

Mary

On June 29, the train stopped opposite Fort Kearney, a military post on the south bank of the Platte. The fort was established in June, 1848, and was located approximately eight miles south of the present-day town of Kearney, Nebraska.[14] It was an important post, providing protection for travelers on the Overland Road. It was not a supply post for emigrants, however, and thus the Edgertons decided not to cross the river to visit the fort.

July 1 marked their first month away from home, and Mrs. Sanders observed: "Have had a pleasant journey and better health than I expected. Hope I can write the same at the end of the month."[15] On July 4, Mrs. Edgerton again paused to write a letter home, this time to her mother:

July 4, 1863

[No Salutation]

Just where I am I cannot say, but on the broad prairie somewhere; have just come to a camp where the men are going to the states and will take letters for us. We are all well now. Sidney was sick with croup last Saturday night. Did not have it after that.[16] We had a very heavy rain last Monday night and until noon Tuesday. Mr. E., Wright and Sidney and myself sleep in a tent. Those that slept in wagons were drowned out about eleven o'clock. Hattie called to us to know if she could come into the tent with her children. We told her to come on and just as we got fairly fixed in bed, Lucia, Mattie and Pauline came in. We made out to squeeze Pauline into the bed with us. The rest made out to find places to sit down. The rain was pouring down in torrents accompanied with such thunder and lightening as you never have in Tallmadge. You had better believe we had a great time, but we had a greater

14 See Robert W. Frazer, *Forts of the West: Military Forts and Presidios, and Posts Commonly Called Forts, West of the Mississippi River to 1898* (Norman, Oklahoma, 1965), 87.

15 Sanders Diary, July 1, 1863.

16 Here she refers to her son Sidney. She always refers to her husband as "Mr. Edgerton." The croup was a name given to a childhood respiratory problem that involved a harsh cough.

Martha (Mattie) and Pauline, daughters of Sidney and Mary Edgerton

time the next two days drying our bedding and other things that were wet. We did not any of us take cold.

The weather has been very warm for a week past with the exception of a day or two. I would like to know just how and what you are all doing today. I will bet that you did not have molasses and ginger and water to drink for dinner today. We did, and the water was taken from the Platte river. It is excellent water but not very cold. We have got along finely so far. We have not seen or heard of any Indians for a week past. There is a large train going to Salt Lake with or near us now. I don't know how long we shall keep with them. Their wagons are heavily loaded and they can't travel as fast as we can.

I do not get much time to write. Can't write much more now for the men are ready to start. Have not written half that I would like to and don't know that you will ever get this. I wish we could

21

get letters from home. Do write as often as you can, — all of you. I will send this to Mother but it is for you all. I meant to have written to Abbie and William[17] before this but really I do not [get] any time to write for we have all we can do after we stop at night and before we start in the morning without writing. When we get to our journey's end I will write to them. Tell the children that we saw four buffalo the other day and have seen a good many antelopes (all at a distance) and any number of prairie dogs and gophers.

Well I must stop. I have written in such a hurry that I am afraid you cannot read it. We may have one chance to send letters before we get to Fort Laramie. Goodbye. Love to all.

Mary

On July 11, the caravan sighted Chimney Rock, a tall perpendicular column that rises out of the plains on the south side of the Platte near the present-day border of western Nebraska. Several members of the party waded across the river and walked for two hours in the hot sun to visit the site. They climbed part way up the rock, broke off a small piece for a souvenir, and then walked back to join the rest of the party.

On July 21, the Edgerton party reached the vicinity of Fort Laramie, just inside the present border of Wyoming, in what was then the Idaho Territory. It was originally erected in 1834 as a fur trading post and was the only significant stopping point on the Edgerton's route between Omaha and Bannack.[18] On that day, they stopped some three miles short of the fort to clean up and to make preparations for visiting there. They camped near a large settlement of Indians and several of the Indians visited their camp, begging for food. Several members of the train attended the funeral of an Indian squaw while others rode ahead into Fort Laramie to pick up mail that had been sent to them in care of the fort. Mrs. Edgerton remained in camp and upon receiving the mail wrote a letter home:

[17] Abbie and William Chandler of Parma, Michigan. Mrs. Chandler was Mrs. Edgerton's sister.

[18] See Frazer, *Forts of the West*, 181–82.

Fort Laramie, Idaho Ter.
July 21, 1863

Dear Sister,

We received your letter written July 1st today. It is the first time that we have heard from any of you since we left Omaha five weeks ago today. We did not go to Kearney so if there were letters directed to that place we shall not get them. We have come to this place fully as soon as we expected to. We are camped about six miles from Laramie. I don't know how long we shall stay here. Mr. E., Wilbur and Mr. Gridley went into Laramie today. Mr. E. has not got back yet — but expect him soon. Lucia, Hattie, Mattie, and Henry have [gone] to see a squaw buried. I presume Mattie will give Mary an account of it.

We have had some very warm days and some very cold days this month. We have all been well until last Sunday, [when] Wright had one of his attacks of severe colic which lasted through the day and [he] had fever at night. He is well now. I have had a hard headache today but feel better this afternoon. I wish I could give you a description of a trip that Mr. Edgerton, Mattie, Wright and Almarette Geer took last Friday. (Lucia will if she gets time give to Ben[19] an account of her trip to Chimney Rock last Thursday.)[20] We went or started to visit Scott's Bluff about twenty miles this side of Chimney Rock.[21] It did not look as if it were more than two miles from camp. Well, we started a little before eleven o'clock, Mattie on the pony, the rest of us walking. (You must remember that we are on the north side of the river Platte and these sights are on the south side.) We walked about half a mile then took off our stockings and shoes and waded across the river. We were nearly an hour in crossing; the river was very wide there but there were many sand bars that we could rest on. Mattie managed the pony very well [and] did not get into the quicksand very badly. In some

[19] Benjamin Wright was Mrs. Edgerton's brother.

[20] Miss Darling noted in her diary that "with much fatigue we reached the rock at last after more than two hours fast walking and commenced ascending the sloping rocks leading to the upright chimney . . . . [We] pulled ourselves up by our hands and feet till we reached the foot of the chimney where we expected to find the names of friends who had passed here and carved their names on this rock in 1850 and thought we would leave ours but did neither as there was such a sea of names there already on every face of the soft rock that could possibly be reached . . . . It seems really wonderful what convulsion of nature could have placed that perpendicular column in that place apart from others of its kind." (Darling Diary, July 16, 1863.)

[21] Scott's Bluff is on the south side of the Platte River, just inside the western Nebraska border. It was named for Hiram Scott, a fur trader who died at the bluff.

places the water was only a few inches deep and then it would be two or three feet deep.

When we started from the river, the Bluff looked about as far as Mr. Shaw's[22] house is from the store. We walked three-quarters of an hour and came to a road and there was a train going to Omaha. Mr. E. stopped to talk a moment with the head man and asked him how far it was to the Bluff, and said that we were going there. The man laughed and said that it was six or seven miles. We would not believe it possible and said we would go anyway and started on and walked until after two o'clock and found [that we] were not getting much nearer and there was a thunder shower coming up and so we concluded to turn back so that we could cross the river if possible before it should rain. The shower came up very fast and we only had time to get to the first sand bar before it came in all its fury. And such a storm. It was almost a hurricane. Imagine if you can Mr. Edgerton standing holding the pony, the rest of us sitting on the sand as close together as we could and hail and rain coming thick and fast and the wind blowing a perfect gale. I will confess that <u>I</u> was afraid of being blown into the river. The storm lasted half an hour. We then went back and went further down the river to cross where it was not as wide. Mr. E. laughed at me for being afraid to go into the river, but in some places the water was up to our waists. You won't have much of an idea what a time we did have from what I have written. I only wish you could have seen us. We got back to our wagons after four o'clock.

We have passed through some splendid scenery. Ben will remember some of the bluffs on the south side of the river, they are not as fine on this side, still there are some very fine ones. I wish you could see them. I have saved some seeds of the sensitive plant. I don't know when they ought to be sowed. I will sow a few this fall and the rest next spring. I will send you seed of a beautiful white flower that blossoms in bunches like the verbena. That is a handsome flower. I shall save seed of all the flowers that I can. I have seen a great many beautiful flowers that I will save seed if it ripens soon enough. There are two kinds that I would like to get seed. One is a purple flower about the size of a small tulip and shaped very much like one. It is very beautiful, but I am afraid that the seed will not ripen soon enough. The other flower looks like a large red morning glory but grows on a shrub or bush with leaves like a willow. I would send you some of the flowers but they do not retain their color very well.

[22] Mr. Shaw was married to Mrs. Edgerton's sister Lucy Ann.

July 22. We have just crossed the river and [are] now in Laramie, and cannot have but a few moments more to write. I have not written half that I would like to. We are glad enough to get your letters from home. Remember us to all the folks. . . .

Write often, some of you. We will probably have a number of chances to send letters back between here and South Pass. We will send as often as we can. Mr. Edgerton is ready for the letters so goodbye. Give our best love to Grandma. Tell Alla[23] Pauline will answer her letters as soon as she can.

Mary

After leaving Fort Laramie, the party drove a few miles and camped for the night. Until this point, the road had been fairly flat and had presented no real obstacles to their travel. However, at this point the small train came into the foothills of the Rocky Mountains and travel became more difficult. On July 29, Mrs. Sanders complained that "We have passed over the worst, the highest, the steepest hills and pitches that I ever saw." [24] By now the trip was beginning to take its toll and patience was wearing thin. Lucia Darling observed: "We had been told before we started . . . that we should need to lay in a good stock of patience but had no idea that such a quantity was needed. Little faults grow to be immense in the sight of the others at times and such a spirit of contention seldom exists." [25]

On Friday, July 31, they came to Deer Creek Station, a small military post and telegraph station. There they sent and received letters, and Mrs. Edgerton wrote a short note home:

Deer Creek Station
July 31, 1863

Dear Sister,

I have but a few moments to write before the wagon starts again. I think we are near Platte Bridge but don't exactly know our whereabouts.[26] We are all well and doing well. Nothing of

[23] Alla Carter was Mrs. Edgerton's niece.

[24] Sanders Diary, July 29, 1863.

[25] Darling Diary, July 29, 1863.

[26] The Platte Bridge was originally built in 1852–53. It was located at the site of present-day Casper, Wyoming. At this point, the wagon road crossed the North Platte and ran for a few miles on the south side of the river. The

Lucia Darling (niece of Sidney Edgerton)

importance has transpired since I last wrote. We came near having a serious accident this morning. As we were riding along Sidney went to get out as he had often done before when the wagon was moving. He made a misstep and fell down in front of the wheels but he drew himself back under the wagon and kept still until the wagon had passed over him. By so doing he escaped unhurt.

I have just found out that we are at Deer Creek Station. We have lived well this week. One of our party killed a deer last Monday and yesterday we killed six grouse and we are going to have pot pie for dinner. Don't you wish you could have some? We are coming to where there is plenty of game. I cannot have time to

Edgertons came to the bridge on August 3, but did not cross it. Instead, they simply drove their wagons through the shallow water. (Sanders Diary, August 3, 1863.)

write longer this morning for the teams cannot wait for me. I may have a chance to send another short letter at Platte Bridge. I will write as often as I can if I do not write but a few lines.

We are having cool weather, it is very pleasant but the nights are <u>very cool</u>. Our provision is lasting well. We have just used the last of Hattie's butter, it kept very well. I shall open mine today. I would like very much to see you all. Love to all. In haste.

Mary

On August 3, the company suffered its first serious accident, when several spokes broke on Mr. Chipman's wagon. This posed a serious problem, for the party was miles from any blacksmith shop where they might obtain a replacement wheel. Fortunately, someone in the group remembered that two or three days earlier they had passed a broken wheel near the side of the trail. Wilbur Sanders immediately rode back to find it and returned the next day with eight spokes. With these, the men were able to repair Chipman's wagon, and after a delay of twenty-four hours, the train resumed its journey.

On August 5, they bade farewell to the Platte River in what is now central Wyoming, and turned up the valley of the Sweetwater. Mrs. Sanders left the river with some regret and noted: "We have camped on its bank so many, many days and drank of its waters that it seems like an old friend and I feel bad to leave it." [27] On the next day they camped for the first time on the Sweetwater River, about 100 miles east of the South Pass, at the foot of Independence Rock, a huge formation some 140 feet high and 2,000 feet long. Mrs. Sanders termed it "the grandest rock in the world," while Lucia Darling described it as "a stupendous formation." [28] It was one of the prime "tourist attractions" on the Overland Trail; thousands of passing emigrants scratched their names on it. Several members of the party climbed to the top of the rock, and while camped at its base, Mary Edgerton began her last surviving letter home from the journey west:

[27] Ibid., August 5, 1863.

[28] Ibid., August 7, 1863; Darling Diary, August 7, 1863.

At the foot of Independence Rock
August 6, 1863

Dear Folks at Home,

Benja. can give you some description of this great rock. I wish you could all see it. It is a grand sight. Mattie and Wright and Sidney have gone to see if they can climb up on it. It is so near night that I think they will not succeed in getting very far up it. I have just been looking and I see Mattie and Almarette on the very summit.

The scenery here is very fine. I wish you could have been with us. Day before yesterday we were obliged to stop because a wheel broke on one of our wagons. We camped at the Red Buttes (pronounced butes.) They are large bluffs of bright red sandstone. If Ben saw them he will remember them for they look so singularly beside the other bluffs. There are three of them; there we bid farewell to the Platte River. I for one was very sorry to do so for I felt as if we were leaving a good friend. When we first came to it the water was very muddy and I thought that I could never drink it but I have learned to like the taste of it better than any water I ever tasted (it would settle very readily). It was very sweet and now is very clear and cold. We are now travelling up the Sweetwater River. It is a much smaller stream than I had supposed it was; it is not much larger than the Little Cuyahoga, but the water is clear and cool.

Friday, Aug. 7. I meant to have finished this today but had to do our washing and did not get time. We travelled ten miles this afternoon. Six miles from Independence Rock is Devil's Gate. When we got opposite it we stopped our team and all went to see it. It is the grandest sight that I ever saw. It is worth our journey here, just to see it. The space or chasm is over one hundred feet wide and the walls of rock on either side are four hundred feet high. Then the river turns, tumbling through the rocks and making a good deal of noise. Oh, it is a grand sight, but one that ought to be seen to be fully appreciated.

Sat., August 8th. We have come eighteen miles today and camped on the bank of the Sweetwater River at the foot of large bluffs. The roads are generally pretty good but dusty. There are some pretty bad hills but not as many as I expected to find. We have not had a drop of rain or dew for weeks.

The air here is filled with electricity. When I bring in my clothes after washing they will snap and crackle more than any woolen cloth ever does with you in winter. In the night when I rub my fingers across the comforter, streaks of fire will follow as when you rub a match to light it. I have thought of Dr. Sales and thought if he was living how much good this dry atmosphere would benefit him. We have sent a number of letters home during the last few weeks. I don't know whether you will get them or not. I wish we could get letters from home as often as we send.

I suppose you are now feasting on ripe fruit of different kinds and vegetables of all sorts. I would like to take dinner with you and help you eat them. I think I should relish a boiled potato, but don't know but that it might make me sick. We have fresh meat often but vegetables are hard to get. We find two kinds of currants that are very good to eat but bitter sweet. I will send you some seed in this letter. I don't know whether any of them will grow or not. I have some other seeds but don't know anything about the flower so will not send them. We do not see any flowers now, everything is so dry. . . . We are all well. The children have all grown fat. I wish you could see Sidney. He took my shears, and cut off his eyebrows a few weeks ago, and it does make him look funny enough. They are beginning to grow out again now. I thought that I should have time to write another sheet but I can't. . . . I will write again before long to mail at [the] next station. Write often and tell all the news. I sent you a specimen of land that we had to go through today.

Mary

After passing Devil's Gate, the Edgertons began the long climb toward the South Pass over the Continental Divide. The road became more difficult to travel, and the nights became increasingly colder. In mid-August, they reached South Pass. There the party took Lander's Cut Off to the northwest. The route had been surveyed by General Frederick W. Lander in 1857–58 and the Edgertons followed it from the South Pass in south central Wyoming to the Snake River.[29]

Up to this point the Edgertons were still not certain of their ultimate destination. The capital of Idaho had not yet been designated when they left Ohio, and en route across the plains they had heard a variety of rumors as to the site. Finally, on August 15, the

[29] Carl I. Wheat, *Mapping the Transmississippi West, 1540–1861* (San Francisco, 1957–1963), IV, 155–56; see also E. Douglas Branch, "Frederick West Lander, Road Builder," *Mississippi Valley Historical Review*, XVI (September, 1929), 172–87; W. Turrentine Jackson, *Wagon Roads West: A Study of Federal Road Surveys and Construction in the Trans-Mississippi West, 1846–1869* (New Haven, Connecticut, 1964), 193–95.

telegraph operator from the station in South Pass overtook the party and announced that he had just received a dispatch that the capital would be located at Lewiston on Idaho's western border. Mrs. Sanders noted that they "were all glad" to hear the news and felt that "it will be far pleasanter and provisions much cheaper than at Bannack," another rumored possibility.[30]

By this time, the party was beginning to descend the western slope of the Rockies and Mr. Sanders had become ill with a cold. He had a severe headache and a high fever, the first real illness suffered by any member of the caravan. Over the next few days he rested while Mrs. Sanders fed him hot tea and Dovers Powder, a drug made from opium and ipecac which was administered to reduce pain and to induce perspiration. The illness lasted several days and then he gradually began to improve. The group counted themselves extremely lucky in this respect, for en route they had passed the graves of several emigrants who had died on the plains from the strain of the journey and due to lack of proper medical care.

The roads through the mountains became increasingly treacherous, although the scenery improved dramatically — "far grander than anything we have passed before." [31] As the nights grew colder, water and milk began to freeze. Descending the mountains was very difficult and required extreme caution lest the wagons run away down a hill or tip over down a steep mountain bank.

On September 2, the train came to the road to Bannack and the Edgerton party, still intent on going to Lewiston, said goodbye to some of the other emigrants who had joined them on the trail. However, on Sunday, September 6, while at the Snake River Ferry, they decided to change course and go to Lewiston by way of Bannack. Bannack was but 150 miles away, and they estimated that Lewiston was still about 400 miles. That day they met the express from Bannack to Salt Lake City and the expressman told them that the roads to Bannack were good. Consequently, they

[30] Sanders Diary, August 15, 1863.

[31] Ibid., August 24, 1863.

determined to go to Bannack and cross the mountains from there to Lewiston.[32]

On September 7, they crossed the Snake River with some difficulty, and headed north. They made good progress and on September 12, Mrs. Sanders noted that "the roads are good and the weather delightful. . . . We are only a hundred miles from Bannack where we expect to stop for a few days at least." [33]

The road to Bannack left Lander's Cut-off north of Fort Hall, south of present-day Idaho Falls, Idaho, and then went over Monida Pass.[34] Thus the Edgertons crossed the Continental Divide for a second time and descended into the valley of the Beaverhead River. Finally, at three o'clock on Friday, September 18, they reached the top of a hill and saw Bannack stretching below. Lucia Darling remembered that "the view was not an inspiring one. There were a few log houses of varying size and description. In the distance, the most conspicuous sight was the gallows." [35] Looking down on the city, five-year-old Jimmie Sanders pronounced: "Bangup is a humbug," and no one disputed the observation as the men of the party locked the wheels of their wagons for the descent down into the camp.[36]

[32] The journey to Lewiston via Bannack City would have been a difficult one. Alonzo Leland's "New Map of the Mining Regions of Oregon, and Washington Territory" (1863) does show a road running northwest through the Big Hole country to Fort Owen then on north to the "Lt. Mullan Road to Fort Benton," which proceeded west and south to Walla Walla. A road then ran east to Lewiston. This would have been an extremely circuitous route. (See Wheat, *Mapping the Transmississippi West*, V, 98.)

[33] Sanders Diary, September 12, 1863.

[34] J. L. Campbell, *Idaho: Six Months in the Gold Diggings, The Emigrant's Guide Overland* (New York, 1864), 50, gives the following description of Lander's Cut-off, located four miles west of South Pass and 765 miles from Omaha. "Here the party leave the California trail, if they wish to go via Lander's Cut-off, and take the right hand road."

Two hundred and four miles farther, at Blackfoot Creek a road branched to the right which led to Snake River Ferry. Proceeding along this road for 54 miles, travelers reached Snake River Ferry owned by Harry Richard. The route then proceeded along the west bank of the Snake River, along Summit Creek, Johnson's Springs, and Horse Creek Ranche to Bannack City — a distance of 137 miles from the Snake River Crossing.

For a full treatment of the Lander Cut-off see Peter T. Harstad, "The Lander Trail," *Idaho Yesterdays*, 12 (Fall, 1968), 16–28.

[35] Darling Diary, Appendix.

[36] Ibid.; Sanders Diary, September 18, 1865.

Chapter 2

Bannack, 1863–1865

S THE EDGERTONS looked down over Bannack, they viewed a town that was barely a year old. It had been the first gold camp of any significance within the borders of present-day Montana, but already, by mid-1863, it had begun to decline in importance.

Gold had been discovered there on July 28, 1862, by John White, a disappointed prospector from Colorado who was passing through the area en route to the Salmon River mines on the western side of the Rocky Mountains. He made his strike on Grasshopper Creek, a tributary of the Beaverhead River on the eastern side of the mountains in the southwest corner of what is now Montana.

White's discovery was not the first in Montana, but it was the first to attract a sizable crowd. Word of the strike spread quickly and eager prospectors headed for the new diggings. The first miners to reach the area began a small settlement on the north bank of the creek, a few miles above the site of White's original discovery. As was customary in mining regions, they held a series of meetings, adopted a list of rules and regulations for their own governance, and named the place East Bannack after the Bannock Indians who frequented the area and to distinguish it from West Bannack, a camp on the other side of the mountains. Later, they changed the name to Bannack City.[1]

[1] The discovery of gold at Bannack is detailed in most general histories of Montana. The best of these are K. Ross Toole, *Montana, An Uncommon Land*

Bannack City (capital of Montana Territory) in the 1860s

At the outset, the Bannack mines were placer mines; at this point, using a variety of techniques, the miners were able to "wash out" free particles of gold from the gravel along the banks of the stream or from its bed. Placer mining was hard work, but it required few tools and only a minimum amount of technical knowledge. However, some of the gold was not loose, but lay imbedded in rock formations known as lodes. This gold could not be washed out, but had to be secured by a process known as quartz mining, in which the rock was first crushed and the gold then separated by a chemical process. Quartz mining required machinery, labor, capital, and technical know-how possessed by few placer miners. Several quartz lodes were discovered in the Bannack area, and in the winter of 1862–63, two miners built a stamp mill —

(Norman, Oklahoma, 1959); Merrill G. Burlingame, *The Montana Frontier* (Helena, Montana, 1942); James M. Hamilton, *From Wilderness to Statehood: A History of Montana, 1805–1900*, edited by Merrill G. Burlingame (Portland, Oregon, 1957); and Merrill G. Burlingame and K. Ross Toole, *A History of Montana* (New York, 1957). The mining laws of the Bannack district are detailed by A. J. Noyes in his edition of Thomas J. Dimsdale's *The Vigilantes of Montana; or, Popular Justice in the Rocky Mountains . . .* (Helena, Montana, 1915), 222–25.

a machine to crush the rock in which the gold was imbedded. This first Bannack stamp mill was a small, crude device powered by water and manufactured from old wagon parts. But in the years after 1862, quartz mining became an important part of Bannack's economy.[2]

Initially, most miners lived in wagons, tents, or brush wikiups, or simply slept in their bedrolls near their claims.[3] However, with the approach of colder weather, they stopped mining long enough to build more permanent shelters. Most construction was along the north side of the creek, although some buildings were erected on a large area on the south side known as Yankee Flat. Whipsawed lumber was available as early as November, 1862, but, because of its high cost, almost all of the buildings in Bannack were constructed of logs.[4] These structures were small and quite primitive with bare walls, dirt roofs, and in most cases, dirt floors. Still, one Bannack resident described his cabin as "quite cozy and home like."[5]

Between four and five hundred people spent the winter of 1862–63 in Bannack, and of that number, probably no more than fifty were women. A list of Bannack's citizens that winter which is "not entirely complete," indicates a population of 370 men and 33 women. Twenty-two women were listed as "Mrs.," seven as "Miss," and four as "widow."[6] Three principal elements contributed to the population: disappointed Colorado miners who had started for the Idaho mines but who had stopped at Bannack; a group of miners who had heard of the Bannack strike and came over from the "west side" of the mountains; and a group of immi-

[2] See W. A. Clark, "Centennial Address on the Origin, Growth and Resources of Montana," *Contributions*, II (1896), 51; Jack Toole, "The Founding of Bannack, Montana," typescript (MHS); Michael A. Leeson, *History of Montana, 1739–1885* . . . (Chicago, 1885), 217.

[3] Charles S. Warren, "History Address 'The Territory of Montana,'" *Contributions*, II (1896), 63.

[4] Dimsdale, *Vigilantes of Montana*, 203.

[5] Granville Stuart, *Forty Years on the Frontier as Seen in the Journals and Reminiscences of Granville Stuart, Gold-Miner, Trader, Merchant, Rancher and Politician*, edited by Paul C. Phillips (Cleveland, Ohio, 1925), I, 231.

[6] *Contributions*, I (1876), 334–54. See also W. F. Sanders, "Early History of Montana," incomplete manuscript (MHS), 165; and Stuart, *Forty Years*, I, 226, 233.

grants who had come from Minnesota in a government expedition led by Captain James Fisk. About 165 people had come to the area with Fisk, heading for the Salmon River mines in the summer of 1862. On September 5, 1862, the Fisk Party arrived at Fort Benton and heard that the Salmon River mines were overrun but that gold had been discovered on the eastern side of the mountains. The party learned of White's discovery at Grasshopper Creek and dispatched a group to investigate the situation. Upon receiving a favorable report, the Minnesotans moved to Bannack. Eventually, about half of the group continued west with Fisk, while the other half remained on the Grasshopper and thus formed a large part of Bannack's early population.[7]

People who came to the gold fields expected to make their fortunes in a variety of ways. Most were miners, but some were store keepers, saloon owners, gamblers, and dance hall girls who hoped to make money by selling supplies and services of every description to the miners. A few were outlaws, intent on enriching themselves at the expense of those who made money in more legitimate pursuits. Few of these people expected to stay very long, let alone become permanent citizens. The one common goal that most all of them shared was to make their fortunes and return to "the States" and to civilized life as quickly as possible. As one of them later recalled, Bannack was "simply a mining camp where everyone was trying to get what he could and then go home." [8]

A principal concern of the first Bannack residents was the lack of enough provisions to get them through the winter. In early September, a ten-wagon train of supplies arrived from Utah. The train was en route to the Deer Lodge Valley, but hearing of the Grasshopper discovery, stopped at Bannack and sold its goods there. Still, these supplies were not nearly enough, and several members of the Fisk expedition who owned wagons and teams

[7] James Fergus, "Early Mining Life at Bannack and Alder Gulch," *Rocky Mountain Magazine*, I (December, 1900), 265–66; see also James L. Fisk, *Expedition from Fort Abercrombie to Fort Benton*, 37th Cong., 3d Sess., 1862–63, House Ex. Doc. 80.

[8] James Fergus, "A Leaf from the Diary of James Fergus Relative to the Fisk Emigration Party of 1862, and Early Mining Life at Bannack, 1863," *Contributions*, II (1896), 252–54.

began freighting in supplies from Salt Lake City. In addition, Utah businessmen heard of the discovery and sent trains to the settlement. Fortunately, the winter of 1862–63 was relatively mild and there was little snow on the mountain passes. Thus, freight trains were able to operate between Utah and Bannack for most of the winter.[9] The miners were also fortunate in that cattle raising had preceded them to the area and thus fresh beef was available through the winter as was a variety of wild game animals.

Prices in the camp were high, but people generally had all the food and supplies that they needed. Flour sold for as much as $40.00 per hundred-pound sack; sugar, coffee, and bacon were $1.00 per pound. Lumber was 20 cents per foot, nails $1.00 per pound, tea $4.00 per pound. An 8 by 10 inch pane of glass cost $1.00.[10] Merchandising was apparently more profitable than mining, and in April, 1863, one merchant, Granville Stuart, closed up business in Bannack and left, having collected "all together about three thousand dollars." [11]

Miners continued to work through the winter as weather permitted. One miner, James Fergus, wrote his wife that the Bannack mines "are not as rich as the Salmon River Mines were, but are far better on the average than Pikes Peak. Miners [are] making an average of $5.00 a day, some as high as $10 and $15. Wages are $4. There is no doubt but we are in an extensive gold country." [12] Approximately $500,000 in gold had been taken out of the area by the end of 1862.[13]

[9] Stuart, *Forty Years*, I, 231; Sanders, Early History of Montana," 156.

[10] See James Fergus letter to the *St. Paul Press*, January 1, 1863 (Fergus Collection, University of Montana Archives); Emmet Nuckolls letter to the *Tri-Weekly Miners' Register* (Central City, Colorado), December 28, 1863 (Bannack Collection, MHS); Emily R. Meredith, "Experiences and Impressions of a Woman in Montana, 1862–1863," typescript (MHS).

[11] Stuart, *Forty Years*, I, 234.

[12] James Fergus to his wife, October 16, 1863 (Fergus Collection, UMA).

[13] Leeson, *History of Montana*, 223; James W. Taylor, *Report of James W. Taylor on the Mineral Resources of the United States East of the Rocky Mountains* (Washington, D.C., 1868), 51; Robert G. Raymer, *Montana, The Land and the People* (Chicago, 1930), I, 189; Clark, "Centennial Address," *Contributions*, II (1896), 49–50.

Although the residents of Bannack kept busy during the winter months, the isolation of their existence weighed heavily on many of them. One of the Minnesota immigrants, Nathaniel P. Langford, observed that "Napoleon was not more of an exile on St. Helena than the newly arrived immigrant from the states in this recess of rocks and mountains." [14] Reading material was scarce and consequently, "old newspapers went the rounds of the camp until they literally dropped to pieces. Pamphlets, cheap publications, and yellow covered literature . . . were in constant and increasing demand. Bibles . . . were read by men who probably never read them before." [15]

The settlers especially regretted the fact that news was so slow in getting to their camps. The news that did reach them was always dated and often inaccurate. This was particularly true during the winter months when isolated mining camps could be cut off from the outside world for weeks at a time. During such periods, wild rumors occasionally swept through the communities, particularly regarding the progress of the Civil War. Several times, for example, the news reached Bannack that Washington, D.C., had been captured by the Confederates and that President Lincoln was a prisoner of war.[16] Early in 1863, someone brought a small hand-printing press to Bannack and attempted to start a small newsletter titled *The East Bannack Newsletter*. For some reason, the attempt failed and only three or four issues were printed. None of them survives today.[17]

The lack of regular mail service particularly impressed upon the citizens a sense of isolation. There was no United States mail service to the camp and the mail that went in and out during the winter was carried privately. This service was both irregular and

[14] N. P. Langford, *Vigilante Days and Ways: The Makers and Making of Montana, Idaho, Oregon, Washington, and Wyoming*, edited by Dorothy M. Johnson (Missoula, Montana, 1957), 144.

[15] Ibid.

[16] See Wilbur F. Sanders, "Sketches of Early Settlers in Montana," typescript (MHS).

[17] J. C. Derks, "The First Printing Press that Came to Montana," *Anaconda Standard*, September 5, 1899; see also N. H. Webster, "Journal of N. H. Webster," *Contributions*, III (1900), 300.

expensive. At one point during the winter, for example, a man came into the camp from Walla Walla, Washington, and brought mail with him for the residents of Bannack which he gave to the addressees for $5.00 a letter. Some people could not afford it at those rates and were compelled "to defer purchasing *all* their mail until prices were reduced." [18]

On January 7, 1863, several residents of Bannack drafted a petition to Congress requesting that a mail route be established between Fort Benton and Salt Lake via Bannack. They claimed that they were "in a great measure isolated and cut off from intercourse with our friends and the country at large for want of mail facilities." [19] It would be several months, however, before Congress acted favorably on the matter, and eventually the federal government established Montana's first post office at Bannack on November 21, 1863. Even after that, mail service was slow and unreliable, and some mail was still carried privately.

There were two good fiddlers in Bannack in the winter of 1862–63, "Buz" Caven and Lou P. Smith. Granville Stuart recalled that they held "a number of fine balls attended by all the respectable people and enjoyed by young and old alike." The men put on the best clothes that they had, mostly "flannel shirts with soft collars and neckties." Stuart insisted that "these dances were very orderly; no man that was drinking was allowed in the hall." Men usually outnumbered women at these functions by about ten to one; hence the women had the opportunity to dance every dance. [20]

Freemasonry proved to be another welcome social outlet. In the fall of 1862, a man named William H. Bell died, and before his passing he asked to be buried with Masonic honors. A call went out for all Masons in the camp to meet for the occasion, and to everyone's surprise, seventy-six Masons appeared. They immediately laid plans to formally organize a lodge and while waiting for permission to do so, held "frequent social meetings." Masonry

[18] Meredith, "Experiences of a Woman in Montana."

[19] Photocopy of a petition of Bannack citizens (MHS).

[20] Stuart, *Forty Years*, I, 233.

provided "an element by which they not only became the warmest of friends and brothers, but a power for protection and self-defense." [21]

There were, of course, other diversions. These included saloons, gambling houses, dance halls, and houses of prostitution. The saloons were always popular gathering places. Edgerton's nephew, Wilbur F. Sanders, later explained that they filled "a large space in the social and public life of the camps to which nearly everyone was driven for want of other accommodations in which to settle the multiform public questions which vex new communities." In some ways, "their traffic was to be deplored or condemned," but most saloons "were hospitably conducted by well-behaved attendants or proprietors, only a few of them contented to be known as bad." On Saturday or Sunday, the people in these saloons "generally represented fairly those early communities." [22]

Settlers also gathered in the Bannack stores to exchange information or to engage in idle gossip. One of the most popular places in Bannack was George Chrissman's store which Sanders described as "the news bureau, the university, the social settlement of the hamlet to which intelligent, genial companionship and a wide fireplace gave cheerful welcome." Chrissman opened his establishment in 1863 and "around his blazing hearth the battles, sieges, philosophies, discoveries, personalities, [and] tragedies came under review." "Of course," Sanders noted, "these audiences were composed wholly of males." [23]

In addition to the more law abiding elements of the population, the attraction of the new strike also lured into Bannack a number of "roughs" who heretofore had plagued the goldfields on the western side of the mountains. One pioneer recalled that "vile men and bad women, long emancipated from the restraints of home,

[21] Address Delivered before the Grand Lodge of Montana at its Third Annual Communication, in the City of Virginia, October 8, 1867, by N. P. Langford, R. W. Grand Historian," copy (MHS). See also Cornelius Hedges, "Early Masonry in Montana," *Rocky Mountain Magazine*, I (September, 1900), 13–17.

[22] Sanders, "Early History of Montana," 217.

[23] Ibid., 169; Sanders, "Sketches of Early Settlers in Montana."

and the refining influences of virtuous society . . . had come to Montana full of wicked plots and dark deeds." [24]

Though relatively few in number, the outlaws achieved a degree of organization under the leadership of Henry Plummer, a New Englander who came to Bannack via California, Nevada, and the camps on the west side, leaving a trail of crime behind him. Despite all of his faults, however, Plummer had a winning personality. Even his enemies admitted that he was "cool and dispassionate. . . . He possessed great executive ability — a power over men that was remarkable, a fine person, polished address, and a prescient knowledge of his fellows — all of which were mellowed by the advantages of a good early education." [25]

Plummer arrived in Bannack in December, 1862, and initially managed to please everyone. On the one hand, he ingratiated himself with the more respectable elements of Bannack society, but at the same time he maintained close ties with the unsavory characters who wintered in Bannack and who looked to him for leadership.

Plummer himself was a party to one of the first significant incidents of violence in Bannack when he shot and killed another of the outlaws, Jack Cleveland. The two had come to Bannack together and Cleveland knew of Plummer's checkered past. Moreover, they had been rivals for the affections of a young lady whom they had met en route to Bannack. As the two grew further apart, Cleveland threatened to expose Plummer, and consequently, on the afternoon of January 14, 1863, Plummer provoked Cleveland into an argument in a saloon and shot him. Cleveland died a short time later in the home of Hank Crawford, a local butcher. No action was taken against Plummer. [26]

A more serious incident occurred a week later. A group of Bannock Indians had camped south of Yankee Flat. One of the

[24] Lyman E. Munson, "Pioneer Life in Montana," *Contributions*, V (1904), 201.

[25] Langford, *Vigilante Days and Ways*, 97.

[26] Ibid., 98–100; Thomas J. Dimsdale, *The Vigilantes of Montana; or Popular Justice in the Rocky Mountains* . . . (Norman, Oklahoma, 1953), 28–30. All further references to Dimsdale are to this edition. See also the Diary of James H. Morley, January 14 and 21, 1863 (MHS).

roughs named Reeves had purchased a squaw from the Bannocks but she left him, claiming ill treatment. When she refused to return to him, on Tuesday, January 20, Reeves and two other men named Moore and Mitchell went to the camp and opened fire into an Indian teepee, killing three Indians and a Frenchman who was living with them. They wounded several others.

The killings excited "great indignation" among members of the community.[27] The Indians were "inoffensive, doing no one any harm, and living among us by virtue of an understanding or treaty" that had been made with the Indians the previous fall.[28] Moore and Reeves fled for fear of reprisals, and Plummer fled with them, afraid that in their anger, the citizens might now hold him responsible for the death of Cleveland. A group of citizens was sent in pursuit, however, and arrested the trio some twelve miles from town.

The three were brought back and along with Mitchell tried by jury in a miners' court. Under the provisions of the district regulations, Hank Crawford, the butcher, was appointed sheriff. Plummer was tried first and quickly acquitted on grounds of self-defense after witnesses testified that on several occasions Cleveland had threatened to kill him. Moore, Reeves, and Mitchell were tried the day after Plummer and the whole town turned out to see it. Public opinion ran strongly against the defendants, but during the course of the trials, friends of the roughs circulated freely among the jurors, threatening reprisals if the men were convicted.

Nathaniel P. Langford sat on the jury and later recalled that all of the jurors agreed that the men were guilty of murder, but feared for their own safety if they voted for conviction. Consequently, only Langford voted for the death penalty; the other eleven jurors voted against it. In the end, a compromise was reached and the three were sentenced to banishment from the area. In disgust, Langford termed the affair "the broadest farce." Another witness lamented that "the miners had no head, no leader,

[27] Sanders, "Early History of Montana," 165.
[28] Fergus, "Leaf from the Diary," *Contributions*, II (1896), 253–54.

and no one who could instill confidence in the masses." [29] Consequently, the murderers escaped any punishment, for a later miners' meeting took pity on them and voted to allow them to return to Bannack. [30]

Several of those connected with the trial did suffer for it later. In particular, Plummer singled out for elimination Hank Crawford who had served as sheriff during the trial. In addition to this offense, Plummer was afraid that Jack Cleveland might have betrayed his past to Crawford before his death at the latter's home. On several occasions, Plummer sought to goad Crawford into a fight, but the butcher always refused, realizing that he was at a disadvantage. Finally, Crawford did leave the territory, but not before he had wounded Plummer in the arm with a rifle.

There were other incidents of violence during the course of the winter and spring of 1863, but the more respectable citizens did little or nothing about it. And they remained remarkably naïve about Henry Plummer, as evidenced by the fact that on May 24, 1863, they elected him sheriff of the district. [31]

The arrival of spring in 1863 signaled a feverish expansion of activity in the Bannack area, and during the course of the spring, a number of miners organized prospecting expeditions to search for new goldfields. James Stuart led a group which left Bannack in April, 1863, to prospect in the Yellowstone Valley and to locate townsites. The party originally consisted of two groups which were to join each other during the course of the expedition. The two groups missed their connection, however, and Stuart led the main party on into the Yellowstone Valley.

In the meantime, the second element of the expedition, consisting of six men, encountered problems with the Crow Indians as they attempted to overtake the Stuart group. The Indians forced this group to turn back, and thus the prospectors set out along a

[29] Langford, *Vigilante Days and Ways*, 111; Fergus, "Leaf from the Diary," *Contributions*, II (1896), 254; Morley Diary, January 20 to January 25, 1863.

[30] Dimsdale, *Vigilantes of Montana*, 33–38; Langford, *Vigilante Days and Ways*, 110–11; Fergus, "Early Mining Life at Bannack and Alder Gulch," 266–67.

[31] Minutes of miners meeting, Bannack, May 24, 1863 (MHS).

route to Bannack which took them near a small stream flowing out of the Stinking Water River, some seventy miles east of Bannack. There, on May 26, two members of the group, Bill Fairweather and Henry Edgar, discovered gold. It was apparent that the strike was very rich and the men then staked out claims, named the place Alder Gulch, and returned to Bannack to secure supplies with which to work their discovery.

As soon as the men began purchasing supplies, rumors that they had made a strike began to fly through Bannack. Consequently, when the six attempted to return to Alder Gulch, they were followed by an immense crowd of miners who dogged their heels and refused to let them out of sight. When it became apparent that they could not escape from the crowd, the Fairweather Party called a miners' meeting and refused to go any farther unless the group promised to recognize the claims that they had staked at the time of the original discovery. The crowd readily assented to these conditions, and on June 6, the crowd broke loose into Alder Gulch. By 4:00 that afternoon, the entire creek had been staked.[32]

Eventually, Alder Gulch was staked out for a distance of twelve miles. Six mining districts were created there and several towns sprang into existence, including Virginia City, Nevada City, Circle City, and Central City. Of these, Virginia City, in the Fairweather District, was the principal center and quickly became the most important town in eastern Idaho. Granville Stuart observed that "Bannack was almost deserted on account of the new diggings on Stinkingwater."[33]

This was something of an overstatement; indeed, for a time Bannack's population increased. But already it had been overshadowed by Virginia City and its neighbors as the Edgertons skidded down the hill to Yankee Flat. The party set up camp on the flat, on the south side of Grasshopper Creek, and Edgerton crossed the creek and walked into Bannack to look over the town.

[32] See Henry Edgar, "Journal of Henry Edgar — 1863," *Contributions*, III (1900), 124–42; Peter Ronan, "Discovery of Alder Gulch," *Contributions*, III (1900), 143–52.

[33] Stuart, *Forty Years*, I, 248.

Probably he found what he expected: a primitive mining camp stretching down a narrow gap in the mountains. The principal business houses were located along the main street which ran roughly from west to east down the gulch along the north side of the creek. As Edgerton strolled down the street, heading east, he passed on his left a stable, then French's brewery, Skinner's saloon, Goodrich's hotel, the A. J. Oliver express office, a blacksmith shop, another hotel, a bakery, a meat market, a grocery store, and another blacksmith shop. About midway down the street, a road ran off to the northeast, through a gap in the mountains and up over a hill toward Virginia City. Looking off in this direction, Edgerton could see Cemetery Hill above the town.

On his right, Edgerton passed another set of stables, Morgan's store, a bakery, a saloon, a Chinese restaurant, George Chrissman's store, another saloon, a meat market, a bowling alley, a hotel, a billiard hall, another bakery, and yet another blacksmith shop. Behind George Chrissman's store was the town jail, constructed in 1862. Virtually all of these buildings were of log construction, although a few of them had wooden false fronts to improve their appearance. Grasshopper Creek ran behind the buildings on the south side of the street, and across the creek were the mines and cabins on Yankee Flat. Interspersed among the buildings mentioned above, on both sides of the street, were numerous cabins and other places of business. Miners' claims and cabins continued on down the gulch for some five miles below the city proper. The mountains overlooking the village were, for the most part, barren of timber, and must have conveyed a strong sense of confinement to many of the miners.

Edgerton quickly discovered that he was to be in Bannack much longer than the few days he had intended. The townspeople informed him that the Mullan Road over the mountains was blocked by fallen trees and that snow had begun to accumulate on the mountain divide. Consequently, the journey to Lewiston would be impossible and the Edgertons decided that they had no choice but to spend the winter in Bannack.[34]

[34] Darling Diary, Appendix; Jackson, *Wagon Roads West*, 262.

Edgerton and Sanders both purchased homes and prepared to settle in for the winter. Edgerton bought a building that had formerly been used as a store . He purchased it at a sheriff's auction ordered by the miners' court of Bannack, and paid $400.00 for it.[35] It stood at the west end of town on the bank of Grasshopper Creek. Just upstream from the house was the narrow log footbridge that crossed over to Yankee Flat. The house was "built of logs thrown together in the rudest manner," and had a dirt roof that turned to mud in rain, hail, or snow, and "trickled through on the occupants." [36]

Originally, the structure was one large room with a kitchen annexed to it, but Edgerton remodeled it to make it more serviceable. He built a rough lumber partition, dividing the front of the house from the rear. He then divided the rear portion laterally into two more rooms. The front room served as a combination living room and bedroom, and one corner was curtained off for use

Home of Montana's first territorial governor

[35] The indenture conveying the property to Edgerton is in the Bannack File (MHS).

[36] Martha Edgerton Plassman, "Residence of Montana's First Governor," typescript (MHS); Darling Diary, Appendix; Martha Edgerton Plassman, "Reminiscences," typescript (MHS); Plassman, "Judge Edgerton's Daughter," 113–16, 133.

by Edgerton as his office. The two remaining rooms were bedrooms. There was a stone fireplace on the east wall of the front room, "constructed in such a manner as to carry most of the heat up the chimney." [37]

The only other fireplace was in the kitchen annex and apparently was intended to serve as a stove. The Edgertons found this unsatisfactory, however, and did not use the kitchen fireplace. Instead they installed their sheet iron campstove in the kitchen. The front room fireplace and the cooking stove provided the only source of heat; consequently, the cabin was very cold in the winter.[38]

The Edgertons had brought some mattresses from Ohio, but other than that, they had come without furniture. They expected to be able to buy furniture in Lewiston, but were unable to find any in Bannack. They could buy only a bedstead and two or three chairs, and had to improvise the rest. They nailed bunks to the walls and made the rest of their mattresses using ticking filled with hay or straw. The kitchen also served as the dining room and Edgerton constructed a dining room table with benches instead of chairs to sit on. There were no cupboards in the kitchen, only bare shelves, and even when entertaining, the family of Idaho's chief justice ate off tin dishes and cups they had used on the plains — they had nothing else.

There were few windows in the cabin and, of course, there were no indoor toilet facilities. Neither was there a well or cistern in the immediate vicinity; water for drinking, bathing, or cooking came from the Grasshopper. They washed clothes in a wooden tub with a washboard, and used the washtub as a bathtub. At night their only light came from candles and kerosene lamps.

Mrs. Edgerton did the best she could under the circumstances to beautify the house. She covered the walls of the front room with sheets, but did not have enough for the other rooms. All in all, "it was a poor excuse for a house," her daughter later recalled, but "there was no better house in town." After some improvements were made, Lucia Darling felt that the house "seemed very home-

[37] Plassman, "Residence of Montana's First Governor."

[38] Plassman, "Reminiscences."

like and comfortable," but admitted that "when one has been moving for a few months, he is not inclined to be as fastidious as to the style of house he occupies." [39]

For the next two years, Mary Edgerton's world revolved almost entirely around this house, crude though it might have been. Judging by her letters home and by her daughter's recollections, she seldom went far from the house. Bannack remained a man's world, and the few women who intruded actively into it were beyond the pale of respectable society. Women like Mrs. Edgerton "led secluded lives — almost cloistered in their lack of contact with the world outside." There was little visiting between the women of the community; they stayed at home and "generally found plenty to keep them occupied there. . . . Men did most of the shopping, and nearly all the gossipping." Consequently, "the pioneer women missed the home folk more than did the men, as they had no society or amusements to distract their minds." Mrs. Edgerton's daughter concluded: "I could count on the fingers of one hand the number of women we knew in Bannack, and calls were never exchanged between them." [40]

Undoubtedly, the fact that she was pregnant for nine of her twenty-four months in Bannack and the fact that her husband was gone for several months during that period, contributed to Mary Edgerton's social isolation, and probably she was by nature more reserved than many of the other women in the camp. There were "respectable" balls and parties while the Edgertons lived in Bannack, and it would seem that a majority of the women in the town attended these gatherings at least occasionally. But for one reason or another, Mary Edgerton does not appear to have gone to any of them. In part, this may also have resulted from her religious upbringing. Her daughter recalled that in Tallmadge, "dancing was taboo. . . . [and] neither of my parents believed in public dances." [41]

[39] Plassman, "Judge Edgerton's Daughter," 116; Darling Diary, Appendix.

[40] Martha Edgerton Plassman, "Return Journey," typescript (MHS); Martha Edgerton Plassman, "Pioneer Amusements," typescript (MHS); Martha Edgerton Plassman, "Excerpts from Letters of Mary Edgerton, 1863–1865," typescript (MHS).

[41] Plassman, "Judge Edgerton's Daughter," 144.

Mrs. Edgerton did enjoy visiting with Hattie Sanders who lived nearby until the Sanders family moved to Virginia City in January, 1864. She read available books and newspapers, and her daughter says that this was her "chief amusement." [42] Also, she was very fond of flowers and enjoyed the wild flowers that covered the foothill opposite their house. These "almost took the place of the cultivated ones in which she formerly delighted." [43]

On Thanksgiving Day, 1863, Sheriff Plummer invited Mr. and Mrs. Edgerton, Mr. and Mrs. Sanders, and other Bannack notables to dinner at the house of his sister-in-law, Mrs. Vail. Some two weeks earlier, Edgerton's nephew, Henry Tilden, had been held up by highway robbers, and Tilden insisted that Plummer was one of the road agents. Sanders and Edgerton indicated some skepticism about the boy's identification, and if they had reservations about Plummer, those reservations did not deter them from accepting the invitation. They attended the dinner and feasted on turkeys brought in from Salt Lake at a cost of $40.00 apiece. [44]

Sometime during this early period, a minister named Carr appeared in the settlement. Someone made arrangements to use a building on Yankee Flat for church services, and Carr began preaching to the few people who cared to attend. There was only one hymnal and the sermons "were not exactly what might be termed finished productions." [45] Lucia Darling observed on one occasion that "our minister is not such a one as I wish he was and those few who attend go more from a sense of duty than anything else." [46]

Later, other ministers appeared, but it is unclear just how often services were held in Bannack, for initially, religion did not attract large numbers of people on the Montana frontier. Instead, Sundays were usually reserved for recreational and business purposes. One early merchant noted: "I believe there is [*sic*] more goods

[42] Plassman, "Pioneer Amusements."

[43] Martha Edgerton Plassman, "Retrospect, Summer," typescript (MHS); Plassman, "Judge Edgerton's Daughter," 35.

[44] Plassman, "Judge Edgerton's Daughter," 119.

[45] Ibid., 134.

[46] Lucia Darling to Martha Carter, November 20, 1864 (Edgerton Family Papers, MHS).

sold on Sunday than on all the balance of the week. The miners appropriate Sunday to do their trading and merchants and shop-keepers seem quite willing to accomodate them." [47]

Another immigrant, J. K. Miller, commented that in Virginia City, "there was nothing visible to remind a person in the slightest that it was Sunday. Every store, saloon and dancing hall was in full blast. Hacks running, auctioneering, mining, and indeed every business is carried on with much more zeal than on weekdays." [48] Lucia Darling wrote that in Bannack "when I come and go to church . . . I can see card and billiard playing and all the follies carried on during the week have no intermission on Sunday." [49]

Mary Edgerton occasionally attended services, and carried to Bannack a letter from her old pastor stating that she was a member in "full and regular standing" of her church in Tallmadge and recommending her "to any church of Christ, wherever her lot may be cast." [50] But no doubt she often must have wished on Sundays that she could have been back in her church in Tallmadge.

For the children, things were better. They played with some of the other children of the town and amused themselves in a variety of ways. In the winter, for example, they could slide down the hill opposite the Edgerton home, using dried buffalo hides for sleds. Also, they could slide on the ice that formed on the Grass-hopper. This last could be dangerous, however, and at least one little boy drowned when the ice gave way. Pauline Edgerton narrowly escaped drowning when she fell through the ice. In the spring and summer, the girls picked flowers or went on berrying excursions, while the boys made up games to amuse themselves. On at least one occasion, the children attempted a stage play. On Saturday, October 16, 1864, they offered for the community a production of *King Edward IV*, starring J. A. Hosmer as Edward

[47] Thomas Conrad to his wife, July 23, 1864 (Conrad Papers, MHS).

[48] James K. P. Miller, *The Road to Virginia City: The Diary of James Knox Polk Miller*, edited by Andrew F. Rolle (Norman, Oklahoma, 1960), 77.

[49] Lucia Darling to Martha Carter, November 20, 1864 (Edgerton Family Papers, MHS).

[50] Letter of Carlos Smith, Pastor, May 26, 1863 (Edgerton Family Papers, MHS).

IV, Pauline Edgerton as the Duke of York, and Wright Edgerton as Henry VI.[51]

Mrs. Edgerton felt keenly the lack of educational opportunities for her children in Bannack. There was, of course, no public education of any kind. A Mrs. Zoller had taught a subscription school in Bannack during the summer of 1863, and in the fall, shortly after their arrival, Lucia Darling opened a school in the all-purpose front room of the Edgerton home. The students brought their own books from home and sat at makeshift desks. The number of students was small and the term lasted only until the onset of cold weather when it became impossible to continue. School began again in the spring and ran until summer vacation. Before the fall term of 1864, two friends of the Edgertons from Ohio, Charles Sackett and Richard Fenn, built a schoolhouse on Yankee Flat across from the Edgerton home and the fall term opened there. Eventually about twenty students enrolled.[52] The younger Edgerton children attended the school and Mattie studied alone at home, but Mrs. Edgerton felt that this was a poor substitute for the education they would have received in Tallmadge.

The Indians remained camped nearby, and it seems clear that the settlers considered them to be more of a nuisance than a threat. Indians occasionally visited the Edgerton home, begging or asking questions about a variety of subjects. Mattie Edgerton wrote her grandmother that the Indians of the area were "disgusting-looking creatures." She noted that "as soon as we see them coming we lock the [front] door and pull the string into the kitchen door." They then ignored the Indians who knocked at the doors and peered through the windows, and eventually, "if they find that we do not take any notice of them, they walk off." [53]

[51] Theater Bill (Manuscript Collection, Bienecke Library, Yale University, New Haven, Connecticut).

[52] Darling Diary, Appendix; Plassman, "Judge Edgerton's Daughter," 136; Martha Edgerton Plassman, "Early Schools of Montana," typescript (MHS); Mrs. S. W. Park [Lucia Darling], "The First School in Montana," *Contributions*, V (1904), 187–95.

[53] Mattie Edgerton to Lucy Foster Wright, February 7, 1864 (Edgerton Family Papers, MHS).

The outlaws, however, did continue to pose something of a threat. The Idaho Territory then included all of present-day Idaho, Montana, and much of Wyoming. Technically, of course, Edgerton as chief justice was the principal representative of the Idaho government on the eastern side of the mountains, but there was little he could do about the situation. Federal law provided that he could not assume his duties until he first took an oath of office from someone qualified to administer the oath. No such person could be found and, as a result, Edgerton never did take the oath and qualify as chief justice of Idaho. Even if he had taken the oath, he would have been relatively powerless for he had no United States marshal or any other assistance that he would have needed in dealing with the outlaws.[54]

It is impossible at this point to measure the amount of actual violence in eastern Idaho in 1863, or to assess the effect it had on citizens like the Edgertons. Thomas J. Dimsdale, an early historian of the Montana vigilantes, described the outlaws as "Godless, fearless, worthless, and a terror to the community." Nathaniel P. Langford insisted that "no crime was too atrocious for them to commit, no act of shame or wantonness was uncongenial to their grovelling nature." They were "little else than devils incarnate," and were "insensible to all appeals for mercy, and ever acting upon the cautious maxim that 'dead men tell no tales.' "[55] On the other hand, speaking of Virginia City, Granville Stuart recalled that "there were comparatively few criminal acts considering the way the whiskey and the money flew."[56]

Whatever the case, eastern Idaho was without question rough territory. By late 1863, a criminal element operated throughout the area under the leadership of Henry Plummer who remained at Bannack but who had managed to become sheriff of the Virginia

[54] W. F. Sanders, "Life of Sidney Edgerton" (W. F. Sanders Collection, MHS), 445; W. F. Sanders, "The Beaverhead Country," clipping from an unidentified source (W. F. Sanders Collection, MHS); Sanders, "Early History of Montana," 159.

[55] Dimsdale, *Vigilantes of Montana*, 51; Langford, *Vigilante Days and Ways*, 23.

[56] Granville Stuart, "A Memoir of the Life of James Stuart," *Contributions*, I (1876), 56.

City area as well. Dimsdale says that the number of the outlaws' known victims was 102, and that "scores" of other unfortunates had probably been murdered by the road agents.[57] This estimate is probably high, but has been accepted by most Montana historians as accurate.

Until late 1863, however, virtually nothing was done about the problem. Possibly, the situation did not appear to contemporaries to be as grave as it has seemed in retrospect; perhaps people were simply apathetic in the face of the violence and hoped that if they ignored the problem they could remain personally untouched by it. Certainly, there was little sense of community spirit in the camps; again, most people had come to improve their own economic situation and to get out as quickly as possible. Consequently, they were concerned first and foremost with their own affairs and were correspondingly less concerned with what went on around them.

By late 1863, however, the situation had begun to change, and a few concerned citizens began to take steps on two fronts to alleviate the difficulty. In the first place, a number of citizens were instrumental in the creation of a vigilance committee to deal out summary justice to the road agents.

The immediate catalyst to action was the murder of a young German immigrant named Nicholas Tbalt. In mid-December, 1863, Tbalt's frozen body was found near the wikiup of several ruffians. A hunter took the body to the Alder Gulch camps where there was great public indignation over the killing, and a posse was organized to arrest the outlaws suspected of the murder. Investigation revealed that one of those arrested, George Ives, was probably guilty of the crime. A trial was held before a miners' court and Charles Bagg and W. F. Sanders were chosen prosecutors. One of the other ruffians turned states' evidence and testified against Ives, who was found guilty.

On at least two previous occasions, members of the outlaw band had escaped punishment from the miners' courts, and Sanders was determined that this not happen again. Consequently, he moved for the immediate execution of Ives. The motion carried,

[57] Dimsdale, *Vigilantes of Montana*, 25.

and he was hanged within an hour of his conviction, on December 21, 1863. Shortly thereafter, a vigilante group was formally organized, and within the space of four weeks its members executed an additional twenty-one outlaws, none of whom was given the benefit of a trial. During the course of this action, a group was dispatched to Bannack, and on the evening of January 10, 1864, with the assistance of a hastily formed Bannack vigilante chapter, its members hanged Henry Plummer and his two principal deputies.

On the following day, the vigilantes sought to question a Mexican named Joe Pizanthia who was suspected of being a member of the outlaw gang. As the vigilantes approached his cabin in Bannack, Pizanthia opened fire, wounding two of the vigilantes, Smith Ball and a man named Copely. Ball's wound proved to be relatively minor, but Copely died — the only vigilante to be killed in the process of executing the outlaws.

With the shooting of Ball and Copely, vigilante justice dissolved into mob hysteria. "The popular excitement rose nearly to madness. . . . It was the instant resolution of all present that the vengeance on the Greaser should be summary and complete." [58] Members of the crowd went to the Edgerton home and secured a howitzer that had been left with Edgerton by Captain James Fisk on his 1863 expedition to Idaho. They fired several rounds from the cannon into the cabin, and then stormed it. Pizanthia was found wounded inside, and was dragged out. Just then, Smith Ball returned to the scene and emptied his revolver into the Mexican. Pizanthia was then strung up to a pole and members of the crowd took turns firing at the body. Tiring of this, they then tore down the cabin and set it on fire. They threw the body onto the blaze and watched it burn. Edgerton observed the proceedings from a hill overlooking Pizanthia's cabin, but as the crowd began to tear down the cabin he left the scene. The following morning, prostitutes from the town sifted through the ashes for gold dust that Pizanthia was rumored to have had at the time of his death. [59]

[58] Ibid., 152.

[59] Ibid., 152–54; Langford, *Vigilante Days and Ways*, 297–99; Plassman, "Judge Edgerton's Daughter," 125–26.

The other executions were carried out without resistance and without mob violence, and the level of crime decreased dramatically thereafter. One miner noted in his diary, "since the summary proceedings of the vigilance committee order and quiet prevail throughout the country and one feels as safe, if not safer than in the states." [60] Sanders played an important role in the vigilante movement, but Edgerton felt that because of his position he could not become involved. Sanders kept the chief justice informed of what took place and frequently came to him for advice. [61] Sanders later said that Edgerton gave the movement "his unqualified approval," and that he was "profuse in his expressions of thankfulness that a new era had dawned." [62]

However, not everyone was as enthused about the vigilante movement as was Edgerton. In her introduction to Langford's *Vigilante Days and Ways*, Dorothy Johnson notes that the vigilantes "were bitterly criticized even by other decent men who knew them." [63] Sanders noted that some people objected to the secrecy of the vigilantes and to the fact that they operated in disregard of legal and constitutional principles. One group of opponents apparently tried to organize in opposition to the vigilantes. Sanders argued that these people were friends of the outlaws and consequently the vigilantes banished the group's "two legal advisors and pillars of strength," and then went about their business. [64]

In addition to the vigilante activity, the citizens began to agitate for a division of the Idaho Territory and for the creation of a new territory east of the mountains. Several meetings were held on this subject, money was collected, and several citizens, principally Edgerton, agreed to go to Washington to lobby for the territory's division. [65] Edgerton left Bannack on this errand in mid-

[60] Morley Diary, May 8, 1864.

[61] "Martha Edgerton Plassman Writes Interesting Story," *Great Falls Tribune*, October 23, 1932.

[62] Sanders, "Life of Sidney Edgerton," 446; Sanders, "Early History of Montana," 233.

[63] Langford, *Vigilante Days and Ways*, xvi.

[64] Sanders, "Early History of Montana," 237–38.

[65] See W. F. Sanders, "The Beaverhead Country"; Wilbur Edgerton Sanders, "Montana: Organization, Name, and Naming," *Contributions*, VII

January, 1864, and did not return until mid-summer. Mrs. Edgerton dutifully helped him prepare for the journey which would take him to Washington, D.C., via the family home in Tallmadge. Clearly she would like to have gone with him, but if she had any complaints about the arrangement, she did not commit them to paper.

The most important fact in Mary Edgerton's life as she sent her husband back East was that she was five months pregnant. This probably would have prevented her from making the trip even if it had otherwise been possible. Curiously, there is no mention of her pregnancy in any of her surviving letters home. Perhaps she did not want to alarm her family about her condition, or perhaps she felt that her pregnancy was not a fit subject for the mails, even to her sister. Perhaps she preferred to let her husband deliver the news in person on his arrival in Tallmadge. Whatever the case, her sixth child, a girl whom she named Idaho, was born on May 23, 1864. The doctor who attended the birth "was a stranger to all of us." No regular nurse was available, and so the "Widow Bennett" acted "in that capacity for a brief period." [66]

It is apparent from her letters that Mrs. Edgerton expected her husband back in Bannack before the birth of their child, but he did not return until July 1. Due in part to Edgerton's efforts, Congress divided Idaho and created the Montana Territory with its present-day boundaries.[67] On May 26, President Lincoln signed the bill and a few weeks later, he selected Edgerton to be Montana's governor. Consequently on his return, Edgerton became deeply involved in setting up the machinery of government. He selected Bannack to be the temporary capital, and as directed by the Organic Act that created the territory, he proclaimed October 24, 1864, election day. Under the terms of the Organic Act, during

(1910), 54–55; Helen Fitzgerald Sanders, *A History of Montana* (Chicago and New York, 1913), I, 188; Sanders, "Early History of Montana," 216; *Summit County Beacon*, March 3, 1864.

[66] Plassman, "Judge Edgerton's Daughter," 131; Plassman, "Excerpts from Letters of Mary Edgerton."

[67] The creation of the Montana Territory is described in Hamilton, *From Wilderness to Statehood*, 274–79; and James L. Thane, Jr., "Montana Territory: The Formative Years, 1862–1870" (Ph.D. dissertation, University of Iowa, 1972), 65–85.

its territorial period Montana would be governed by a governor, a secretary, and three judges, all of whom would be appointed by the President. Eligible voters were empowered to elect representatives to a territorial legislature consisting of a council and a house of representatives. In addition, they could elect a non-voting delegate to Congress to represent their views in Washington.

Edgerton faced a very delicate political situation as he entered the 1864 elections, for the Montana electorate represented a kaleidoscope of political attitudes and persuasions. Several diverse elements composed the population, including a group of Republicans led by Edgerton and Sanders. There was a fairly large contingent of northern Democrats. Also included in the population, however, were a number of people from southern and border states. These citizens were in almost all cases Democrats, but beyond that simple assessment, it becomes very difficult to deal with this group. Some of them obviously favored the Union cause. Some clearly supported the Confederacy. A larger element did not actually hope for a Confederate victory, but, like some northern Democrats, did desire a negotiated peace that would allow the southern states to return to the Union with their honor intact.

In Montana, as in the nation generally, Republicans chose not to distinguish among varieties of Democrats. Instead, the Republicans lumped the entire Democratic party together as "copperheads" and accused them of disloyalty. Edgerton, who sought to elect Union (Republican) majorities to the territorial house and council, and to elect Sanders as territorial delegate to Congress, waged a bitter campaign and equated the Democratic party with treason.

In the end, these efforts came to naught. On election day, the voters sent Democrat Samuel McLean to Congress by a margin of three to two: 3,898 votes to 2,666. Sanders won a majority of the votes cast in four counties, but this proved insufficient. The Republican *Montana Post*, the territory's first newspaper, reluctantly conceded defeat, claiming that "the balance of votes in this section [Madison County] were cast by secessionists openly claiming to be citizens of Dixie and voting as citizens of the Northern states." [68] McLean, elected to Congress, was a peace Democrat from Pennsylvania. The Republicans did secure a majority of one in the territorial council; the Democrats secured a similar majority in the house. Almost all of the legislators elected were men from northern states.

One of the representatives elected was John H. Rogers, a popular Democrat from Madison County. When the Civil War broke out, Rogers was a member of the Missouri State Militia. During the summer of 1861, he served under the command of General Sterling Price in an attempt to prevent Union soldiers from entering the state. Later, Price took the militia into the Confederate service. Though willing to defend the neutrality of his state, Rogers was unwilling to take up arms as a Confederate soldier. Accordingly, he left Missouri and joined the Colorado gold rush. In the summer of 1863, he migrated to Montana. [69]

A conflict developed when Edgerton insisted that the legislators take the "Iron-Clad Oath of Allegiance" to the Union, swearing in part, that they had "never borne arms against the United States." [70] Rogers could not take the oath, and hence he offered a substitute of his own, swearing to "support protect and defend the Constitution and Government of the United States and the Organic Act of the Territory of Montana." [71] However, Edgerton would not accept the substitute. He sent word to the House, refusing to recognize it as properly organized until each member had taken the prescribed oath. Rather than force the issue, Rogers resigned.

The meeting of the legislature did lead to a significant improvement in the Edgertons' social life. Their house became a social center during the course of the session, and nightly, delegates and lobbyists crowded into the Edgerton living room to discuss matters before the legislature with the governor, or simply to relax in idle

[68] *Montana Post* (Virginia City), November 6, 1864.

[69] Herbert M. Peet, "Captain Rogers, Rebel Typical of Missourians who Developed Montana," *Great Falls Tribune*, August 7, 1955.

[70] A photostatic copy of the oath signed by all the representatives except Rogers is in the manuscript file (MHS).

[71] Photostatic copy of the oath signed by Rogers, December 15, 1864 (MHS).

conversation or card playing. Sanders noted that "Everybody delighted to go" to the Edgerton home, "where they were received with a graceful hospitality." [72]

Despite some reservations by critics, the legislature produced a number of important measures, including a bill which removed the territorial capital from Bannack to Virginia City. In light of the high cost of living in Montana, the legislature also passed a bill increasing the salaries of the governor and of the justices by $2,500.00 per year, or an increase of one hundred per cent over the salaries paid them by the national government. They also allotted themselves an increase of $12.00 in their per diem allowances.

Two major problems faced the territory at the close of the first legislative session. Edgerton and the legislators had failed to agree on a new apportionment bill, and thus doubts arose over the validity of the territory's legislative functions. The Organic Act provided that the governor should apportion the representation for the first session; the first session was to reapportion itself and thus provide for future sessions. The Act made no provision for its failure to do so, and many Republicans later adopted the position that the legislative functions of the territory had lapsed.

The second and most immediately pressing problem was money. Under the terms of the Organic Act, only the territorial secretary was empowered to sign the warrents disbursing the federal funds designated for the territory, yet Montana had no secretary. Two individuals had refused the office, and only in August, 1865, did President Andrew Johnson appoint a secretary to the territory. In order to keep the government moving, Edgerton supported the first legislature himself, with the help of a few friends, expecting any day the arrival of a secretary who could repay him.[73] As time wore on, Edgerton's patience wore out.

[72] W. F. Sanders, "Notes on Montana History" (Bancroft Collection, Bancroft Library); Plassman, "Martha Edgerton Plassman Writes Interesting Story," *Great Falls Tribune*, October 23, 1932; Martha Edgerton Plassman, "Retrospect, Winter," typescript (MHS); Plassman, "Judge Edgerton's Daughter," 140.

[73] Edgerton to W. H. Seward, January 30, 1866 (Territorial Papers, Montana, Department of State, National Archives); Plassman, "Judge Edgerton's Daughter," 140; Sanders, "Life of Sidney Edgerton," 449.

In addition to the money problem, Edgerton was upset because the government had sent him to the wilderness of Montana and had not sent any laws or instructions by which he might work. In lieu of a secretary, he had been forced to assume all of the secretarial duties himself, except the most vital — that of disbursing the money. In August, 1865, President Johnson appointed Thomas Francis Meagher to be Montana's secretary. However, much to Edgerton's dismay, Meagher arrived in the territory unbonded, and thus unable, even as secretary, to distribute any money.

In view of these grievances, Edgerton decided to leave Montana less than a week after Meagher's arrival, to go back to Washington to appeal for a redress of the situation. This time, he determined to take his family with him, allegedly so that he and Mrs. Edgerton could place their daughter Mattie in school in Ohio.

It is impossible to determine how badly Edgerton wanted to return to Montana. His political career had not been advanced by his presence there, and by mid-1865, he had fallen into disfavor with some elements of the Republican party in Montana. On leaving Bannack, the Edgertons sold their home and their household goods, and in mid-September, 1865, nearly two years to the day from the time that they had come, the Edgertons left Bannack and returned to Ohio.

Upon arriving in Ohio, the Edgertons placed their children in school, and after making the necessary domestic arrangements, Edgerton proceeded to Washington to lay his case before the federal government. His reception was not sympathetic. By the time of his arrival in Washington, Andrew Johnson had become President and was already locked in political conflict with Radical Republicans of Edgerton's persuasion. Edgerton himself conceded that Johnson might wish to replace him with someone else, and when this appeared to be the case, Edgerton resigned in June, 1866, without returning to Montana.

The *Summit County Beacon* noted on the family's return to Tallmadge that "so far as official emoluments were concerned, the Governorship was a losing venture." However, the paper reported that "through mining interests and judicious investments in other enterprises," Edgerton had "secured a sufficiency of *l'oro* to richly repay himself and family for the inconveniences and privations they have suffered." The paper noted that Edgerton had paid $5,000 in cash as a down payment on "the fine property on Medina Street known as the Kilbourn place." [74] The Edgertons were to live in Ohio for the rest of their lives.

[74] *Summit County Beacon*, May 3, 1866. While in Montana, Edgerton had recorded over seventy-five mining claims and had been a partner in at least one townsite company. Most of these claims are in the files of the Clerk and Recorder for Beaverhead County, Montana, in Dillon. It is impossible to determine with any certainty how profitable they were to Edgerton.

Chapter 3

The Letters of Mary Edgerton, 1863

Bannack
Oct. 4, 1863[1]

Dear Mother,

I WOULD MUCH rather be with you today and tell you how we are getting along than to write to you, but I can't be with you, so I will have to write.

We are all living, or staying rather in a house. Mr. Edgerton has bought a very good log house for four hundred dollars. There was nearly enough lumber in it to make all the partitions we shall need. There were only one large room that had been used as a store, and a good kitchen. There are good board floors. Many of the houses have floors made of hides, and many have no floors. Mr. Edgerton has nearly finished. We shall have a sitting room and dining room, and two good sized bedrooms. We shall put a curtain across the end of one of the rooms, for the boys' bed. I think when we get our house finished and things arranged, we shall be very comfortably situated. I like our house. As it is now it is much more comfortable than living out doors, and sleeping in

---

[1] This letter is contained in a typescript titled "Excerpts from Letters of Mary Edgerton, 1863–1865," written by Mrs. Edgerton's daughter, Martha Edgerton Plassman. The typescript is included in Mrs. Plassman's papers at the Montana Historical Society, and quotes from a few of Mrs. Edgerton's letters home. Only this letter is quoted in its entirety. The remaining letters in this edition are from the Edgerton Family Papers, MHS.

tents and wagons these cold nights. If I had known we were coming here, I think I should have left some things I brought, and some that I left should have been brought here. I do not think we could find shovel, tongs, or andirons in the city; if we could they would cost a fortune. Mr. Edgerton paid seven and a half dollars for a pair of flatirons, just like those small ones I left.

Mr. Edgerton had an invitation last week, to visit a claim and "shake a pan of dirt," and got forty dollars of gold dust. As he was coming home, another man who owned a claim nearby, wanted him to shake a pan from his claim. He did so and got thirty dollars. This man was not satisfied with the shake — though he (Mr. E.) did not get enough, and told him to come again next week, and he should shake a hundred dollars next time. I saw a nugget of gold last week worth seventeen and a half dollars.

Monday. I suppose that you have got all through with your washing.[2] We did not wash today, for I want to see if I can get something that will answer for a tub. I bought a small tin tub to use on the plains, which answered the purpose very well, but it is not large enough to wash bedclothes in, and I cannot use my wringer on it.

I presume you have all the fruit you want. Wouldn't I like to help you eat it! If you have dried any fruit of any kind, I wish you would save some for me, so if you have a chance to send it, you will have it ready. We get along better without such things than I ever supposed we could. I have not used all my canned fruit yet — am saving it for extra occasions.

Our butter lasted until about four weeks before we got here, and it kept pretty good too. I am sorry that I did not can some to save until we got here. All the butter used here is brought from Salt Lake, and sells at eighty cents or a dollar per pound. I have not tried any of it yet; we use bacon fat for all our "shortening" and find that it answers the purpose very well. It does not taste smokey as ham fat does, but is more like lard. You may be sure I do not make much cake — I have almost forgotten how it tastes.

[2] Monday was always wash day at home, and Mrs. Edgerton followed this practice of washing on Mondays whenever she could.

Now don't think that I am finding fault because I can't have such things as I have spoken of. We don't think of them very often only when we are talking about the folks at home. We are perfectly contented without them.

You don't know how badly I want to hear from you all. We have sent to Lewiston for our letters, but there is no certainty when we shall get them.

[No signature]

Bannack
October 18, 1863

Dear Sister,

I don't know that I shall have time to write a very long letter to you today but will write as much as I can. It does not seem very much like Sunday here for they do not have any kind of meeting. There is no minister here except a Catholic minister. I think the town is very quiet and orderly for such a mining town — much more so than I expected to find it. We have not got our house finished yet, but hope to soon. I have made my rag carpet and as soon as we can have a fireplace and chimney built, shall put it down on our <u>front</u> room. In looking over our boxes I do not find our oil table spread. I do not remember selling it or of giving it away. I was very much disappointed in not finding it for I was <u>certain</u> that it was packed in one of the boxes. I intended to have brought it. It would be very useful to me. We are all very well now. Wright has been quite unwell until he has grown very poor but he is well now and eats very heartily and his food seems to agree with him.

Before you get this letter you will probably have had "Thanks-giving." We would all like to be with you, but that cannot be, but we shall think of you all about that time, think of what good times you are having. Last week was <u>election</u> in Ohio. Would like to hear the results. It takes news a <u>long</u> time to get here but we value it all the more when we do get it. Have you heard anything from Junius since we left? Have you heard from Edward since the battles in Tennessee? Has he been in any fight yet? When you write to him again tell him that here will be a good place for him when the war closes. He could do a great deal of good here. . . .

Tell Lucy that the fixings that were in that medicine satchel have done us lots of good. I don't [know] what we should have done without them. I think of her whenever I have occasion to use any of them and that is pretty often. . . .

Who teaches the acadamy now? I suppose Mary and Homer attend the school if you have one. How do they get along with their music? . . . I am sorry that Mattie cannot keep along with her music but hope she will improve enough to make up when she has another opportunity to practice. She helps me do the housework now.

Lucia expects to teach this winter, will commence her school this week if she can get a room for her school. Expect to send Wright and Sidney. Mr. Edgerton has just finished a pine table and I tell you we feel proud of it. He is going to make some chairs next and by the time you come to visit us we shall be well supplied with furniture of home manufacture.

I wrote in my last letter to have you save dried fruit (if you have any) for us and if we have a chance to send for some [we] shall do so. I must stop and get supper. Goodby. Love to all.

Mary

Bannack
November 29, 1863

Dear Sister,

I have been waiting for an opportunity to send a letter to Salt Lake or I should have written before. We have to pay a dollar for sending or receiving each letter. Perhaps you will be surprised to see Mr. Edgerton this winter. It does not seem half as far to go back as it did to come here, but it will be a cold and tedious journey. I don't like to think of his going, still I know that it is best that he should go. I hope that Clem will make up his mind to come back with him. It would be a hard journey for Lucy but it might do her good. I wish some of the folks would come out here next summer. We should all be glad enough to see anyone from home. We are all well now. Mattie and Wright have been sick. The rest of us have all been well.

Lucia and Mr. Edgerton and myself had invitations to a Thanksgiving supper. We had an excellent supper equal to any that we ever had in Ohio. I tasted butter for the first time since we came here and it was a treat I can assure you, but as long as it is ten and twelve shillings a pound (and poor at that price) I think we shall do without it most of the time. Everything is very high here. Sugar is 75¢ per pound, pork sixty, flour from twenty-five to thirty, nutmegs 50¢ an ounce &c. &c. I am going to send you a list of things that I would like to have sent if, after Mr. E. gets there and talks the matter over, he should think it best to have them sent. If you should send canned fruit, be sure the cans are firmly sealed so that if the box they are packed in should be turned "bottom side up" they will not come open. When the box is packed, fill in between the cans with sugar or tea so that the cans cannot move either way. If you should send any bottles, put them into tin cans such as you would get ground coffee in and then fill in with sugar. I am afraid that Mr. Edgerton will forget about it so I write to you how to do it.

In sending dry goods, don't send anything nice for I never should wear it here, but send things suitable for everyday wear. The boys have not had on cotton shirts since we left Omaha. Their woolen ones are nearly worn out now but [I] shall try to make them last until Mr. E. gets back. Mr. Edgerton put on a white shirt on Thanksgiving Day for the first time.

We have had some very cold weather but there is one beauty about it. We never have rain and but little snow. How are you all? Who made the Thanksgiving supper this year? We would all like to have been with you. How is Lucy Ann's health now? I suppose you have all written letters to Lewiston. We may get them next year some time but we shall be glad to get them. They will be new to us. How is Lucy now? And all the rest of the folks, are they getting well?

Mr. Edgerton will tell you more in one evening than I could write in all day. I would like to go with him but we can't both leave home at the same time. The winter will seem long but I hope he will be able to come back early in the spring. I should write more letters to send by Mr. Edgerton but I do not get but little time to write many letters so this will have to answer for all. Give my love to all. When you write tell all the news you can think of. . . .

The only large "nugget" that I have I send to Mother. I would like to send one to each of you and would if I had them. This was a present to me for keeping money safely. I send my curls to keep and wear until I call for them. I can't get them recurled here. You will find the "nugget" in the box with the curls and flower seeds. I must tell you that I have just been [making] mince pies and used dried apples instead of green and I think that they are as good as any that I ever made. I can't afford raisins for them but used dried currents. Love to all,

Mary

Sunday
December 27, 1863

[No salutation]

We received letters from you week before last. You don't know how glad we were to hear from home. I have read them over and over. I was glad to hear that you were all well. We are all perfectly well now. Mr. Edgerton now expects to start for the States this week. He has been waiting for a man that owes him, who is at Virginia City. Wilbur is there too, but if he comes in the express today, as we expect, Mr. Edgerton will probably start Wednesday or Thursday in company with a number of others who expect to start at that time. It is not safe now for men to travel alone if they have much money with them. There are too many highway robbers. The vigilance committee at V.C. [Virginia City] is clearing them out some. They hung two men week before last and will probably hang others, so it will be rather safer now than it has been for travellers.

I suppose you all, the children I mean, had great times hanging up stockings on Christmas. Our children did not expect anything but found lots of figs and raisins in their stockings, that Henry got for them. Mattie will write to Mary what she had for presents. Henry gave me a broom. If I had bought it, [it] would have cost $2½, but he being in the express office gets them cheaper. I have written a letter to Abbie to send by Mr. E. and would write to William if I had the time but think it possible that Mr. E. will see him and that will be better than a dozen letters from me.

I do not get much time to do anything but housework, but I will promise to answer all the letters that you will write. Write often. . . . I think your dresses are very pretty. I want you to get something for Lucia and myself, dresses. I hardly know what to send for. I think if you can get cloth like my travelling [dress] of that quality but not that color, it would be what I want. I don't want as expensive cloth as your empress cloth; would like a handsome dark green if you can find it. Get them alike if you can — send lining, whalebones, hooks and eyes and trimming and sleeve patterns, and tell how to make the waist.

Mary

Chapter 4

The Letters of Mary Edgerton, 1864

[No salutation]   January 1, 1864

I WISH YOU ALL a "happy, happy, new year." Wouldn't I like to see you all tonight? I have been very busy today getting things ready for Mr. Edgerton. [I] have been baking gingersnaps, and ironing fine clothes. I am ashamed to have you see his white shirts (I say white shirts because he wears his wollen ones all the time here.) The bosoms look so badly — if I had not so much to do I would wash them over. They are just as I brought them from Omaha.

We received a package of letters from Lewiston this week and have had a "real" feast reading them. You wanted me [to] write how many we received. There were four from you dated June 14, Aug. 2, Aug. 16, and Sept. 8. Mattie had two letters from Mary, Wright one from Willie Fenn and Lucia one from Lucy Ann and Mr. Shaw, one from Mary Ashman and one from Mrs. Sayles. Henry received four. In mine were some for Wright, Sidney and Pauline. I have given one to Pauline and she carries it around in her pocket and takes it out to read very often; it does her, as well as ourselves a great deal of good to get letters. . . .

I don't know how soon Mr. Edgerton will start. It depends on the weather. It has been very cold here for a week past and con-

71

siderable snow has fallen. It has been so cold that the mercury has frozen in the thermometers.

Sunday, Jan. 7th

We received a package of letters from home yesterday over which there was great rejoicing. Letters from home do us a great deal of good. In one of your letters you wonder how I get along without butter? If you were here you would be astonished to see how we get along about cooking without a great many things. I have bought seven lbs. of butter at $1.25 per lb. and expect it to last all winter, but precious little do I use about cooking. I have bought one dozen of eggs at $1.50 per doz. [I] have been without milk most of the time since we have been here; when I do get any [I] have to pay twenty-five cents a quart. I get along very well without it.

I want to tell you how I prepared the juice of lemons so it has kept until now and I presume would any length of time. I bought a doz. of good lemons at Omaha and pressed all the juice into a pitcher, then made it thick with sugar and put it into bottles and corked it tight. [I] put a large spoonful in a tumbler of water and it makes a good lemonade. I used one bottle when Mattie was sick and have one left. The lady that told me how to prepare them said grate the rind of the lemon into the juice but I did not do so for I had no grater. I think it is full as good without. It would taste too strong of the lemon. If you can get the lemons before Mr. E. comes back I wish you would prepare some that way and seal it up and send back to me — you can fix them so for yourself and keep any length of time. Be sure to have good lemons or it will not make good lemonade. Try it. Hattie has just been in and says that I am mistaken about grating the rind into the juice — but that the lady said grate the rind by themselves and put sugar with them and bottle to flavor custards or anything we wished.

I want you to send some school books for the children: Greenleaf's higher arithmetic such as was used in the academy, Town's highest reader for Wright and a geography suitable for him — [a] reader for Sidney and Pauline's primer. Mr. Edgerton says that if he brings back all that we send for he will have to charter a ship, but I don't think so. I have too much faith in Clem's packing boxes.[1] I know that he can put lots into a <u>small</u> box but I <u>don't send for a small box</u>. Tell Mother that she need not send that spread. She or you may have it and do what you have a mind to. I would send you and the rest of the sisterhood a present but there is nothing here that I can buy suitable, so will have to wait until some other time.

I am glad that you have taken good care of little Franky's grave.[2] If Mr. E. does not have time to see to it, in the Spring I wish you could get someone to dig up those rasberry and other bushes by that rock, so that ivy can cover it.

Send me your receipe for making ice cream and I wish I had a small patent freezer but I don't know but it is foolish to send for one.

Love to all

[No signature]

Jan. 17, 1864

[No Salutation]

Mr. Edgerton has not been able to leave here for Washington yet but now expects to start next Tuesday or Wednesday. He got already to go a week [ago] last Friday but it was so very cold that he did not think it prudent to do so, as he would be obliged to go horseback as far as Salt Lake.

The past week has been a very eventful one here. Travelers from here to Virginia City (a mining town seventy-five miles from here) going anywhere, have been very much troubled by highway robbers. A great many have been robbed since we have been here and some have been murdered. A few weeks ago there was a vigilance committee formed at V.C. and a number of these highwaymen were arrested and hung. Before they were hung they made confessions and implicated many others. Their confession was that there was a regularly formed band of them and that the sheriff of

---

[1] Clement Wright was Mrs. Edgerton's brother.

[2] Franky was Mrs. Edgerton's son who died in infancy in Ohio.

this district was the captain. He lived here, was a very feminine-looking man, but the greatest villain of them all.

During the past year they have committed about one hundred murders — and these murders had not been discovered by the people here. The victims were those who had made money and had started for the States. They were murdered and robbed and then their bodies, some of them, cut into pieces and put under the ice, others burned and others buried. A week ago last night four of the vigilance committee came here from Virginia City and told some of the men here what they had learned and what they had done, and wanted to have the people form themselves into a vigilance committee and hang those here that were known to belong to the band. They did so on Saturday night and on Sunday night they arrested three men, Henry Plummer, our sheriff, being one of the number, and took them to the gallows, and hung them.

On Monday they attempted to arrest another of the band — a Mexican — and two of our men were shot by him (one died the next day, the other was not seriously wounded,) which so exasperated the people that they came to our house and got the howitzer that has been left in Mr. Edgerton's care, and with that threw shell into the house which exploded and injured the man. They then took him out and shot and hung him. They then tore down the house and set it on fire and threw the body on and burned it up.

You may think that was hard, but the house had been the headquarters for all those villains for a long time and no one would bury the body. Some were in favor [of] drawing it on to one of the hills near here and leaving it to be devoured by the wolves. Others proposed to throw it onto the burning house, and they did so.

Tuesday they hung another of the band that had been arrested about ten miles from here and brought here, making the fifth that had been hung here, and there have been nine men hung in Virginia City and Nevada, a mining town eight miles from V.C., and they are now in pursuit of others. A number of [men] have been banished from the country on short notice. I hope the Committee will not have to hang anymore here for I do not like such excitement, but I shall feel that Mr. Edgerton will go much more safely <u>now</u>, than he would have gone two weeks ago, for I have no doubt that they intended to have robbed him, for they were very anxious to know when he expected to leave here and how much company he would have, &c., &c. I think that there is no danger of his being robbed now. I do not know how long Mr. Edgerton will be gone, probably three months.

We received letters from home yesterday. They were all well. Martha wrote that she and Mr. Carter had visited you on their way back from Illinois. I was glad to hear it. I was sorry to hear that they had such a lonesome Thanksgiving. I wish they would [not] feel so about our being here. It will not seem so far after Mr. E. has been there. It does not seem half as far for him to go there, as it did for us to come here.

We had extremely cold weather here the week before last. The mercury in the thermometers after going forty degrees below zero froze in the bulb. I never knew such cold weather or anything like it. I was so afraid that the children would freeze their noses or ears in the night that [I] got up a number of times in the night to see that their heads were covered. Their beds would be covered with frost. I saw their frozen breath. It is now much warmer.

Lucia says that she is going to write you before long. We received a package of letters from Lewiston, two weeks ago, but among them did not get any from you. Have you written? There may be other letters there now for these were a long time coming here.

We are all well. Write soon (direct to me care of Judge Edgerton, Bannack City, Idaho Ter.)

[No signature]

East Bannack
Feb. 1, 1864

Dear Sister Martha,

I have been writing to Mr. Edgerton but shall direct his letter to Washington so you will not hear from us unless I write to you.[3] I do not have much news to write. It has <u>seemed very</u> quiet here since Mr. Edgerton left, but I presume there has been as much

[3] Edgerton finally left for Washington on January 21.

going on as usual, only we do not hear of it. I have not heard from Mr. E. since he left — but have been looking anxiously for the Salt Lake express, for a number of days past, thinking that I shall hear from him when it does come. You don't know how lonely I have felt since Mr. Edgerton went away. I know that the rest do not miss him as much as I do.

We have all been very well since I wrote to you last. We have had beautiful spring-like weather until a few days past. It has been colder, but not near as cold as it was before Mr. E. went away. Wilbur's folks have got their things all packed ready for Virginia City. Their things go tomorrow and they will go in the next coach. I expect Hattie and the children to come here tomorrow to stay until the coach leaves. I do not like to have them leave here, but I know that it is better for them to go. It is late so I must stop writing for tonight. Will write some tomorrow if I have time, but have got [to] bake.

Tuesday. I do not remember whether, in the list of things that [I] sent for, I mentioned black spool thread — coarse such as I shall want to use making pants for the boys. Send a number of spools of black and of the browns from number 30 to 40. Send buttons for the coats for the boys. Did I say anything about a looking glass? The only one that we have is that little <u>five cent</u>, round, glass that I bought to carry in my basket. If you could send me one from six to eight inches square it [will] answer our purpose very well.

To tell the truth you <u>can't send anything amiss</u> but I do not expect that <u>all</u> will be sent that I have written for, for they would take too large a box. Send the soda and acid by Mr. E. Soda is $1.00 per lb. and cream tarter $3.00 per pound. It will save us a good deal to have them sent to us. If there is an abundance of room when you pack the things, put in a glass pepper box and salt cellar. I am using tin. I can get glass ones here but they cost so much that I shan't get them at present.

If the new "Lode" which has been discovered since Mr. Edgerton left here, and on which he has claim number 5 from discovery, turns out anything as it is thought it will, we shall be able to have all the glassware that we need a year from now. New discoveries are being [made] here or near here almost every day. Some of them will probably turn out to be rich and others will not be worth much.

But enough of this. I wish you could be here and see what a beautiful day we are having. The weather is so different here from the spring weather that you have; there is none of that chilly feeling when you get out of doors here, that I have always felt when in Ohio. When the snow goes off here the ground does not show it; as soon as it is gone, the dust flies.

Write often as you can. The children send love to Grandma and you all. How is Mother's health this winter? I dreamed that she came and made us a visit. I do not expect that she will do that, but hope that we shall live to see each other again. Love to all. Will write every mail.

Your affectionate sister,
Mary

East Bannack
Feb. 21, 1864

Dear Sister Martha,

I received a good long letter from you last week. You are anxious to know why we have not written oftener. You have probably had it all explained to your satisfaction before this.

As for suffering with the cold, I never knew such extremely cold weather as we had the first week in January, but we manage to keep very comfortable. I used to get up once or twice in the night and go feel the boys' faces to see whether they were frozen or not. The bed clothes would be frozen stiff from their breath, but we did not one of us take cold.

I am glad that you did not lose your plants. Did Lucy Ann lose her oleander? I am astonished that Mother should let her plants freeze — if it had been some of the "girls" I should not have wondered so much. I should like a rose geranium very much, but I do not know as I should succeed in making one grow if I had one.

Our friend, Mr. Thompson, rather unexpectedly starts for the states tomorrow.[4] It is possible that he may bring back a wife with

[4] Francis Thompson was a Republican member of the first Montana territorial legislature and a close friend of the Edgertons.

him. He now expects to see Mr. Edgerton while he is gone, and will probably come back with him. We shall miss him very much, for he has been very kind to us.

The "Union League" are going to have a great "Ball" tomorrow night. I think we shall not attend although we received a complimentary ticket. We shall be apt to hear enough of it, for the Hall that they are going to dance in is right opposite here. I have not heard from Mr. Edgerton since he left here. He started from here on the 21st of January, our birthday.

In your letter you asked about Lucia's health. She never was healthier than she has been since she left Tallmadge. We have all been very well except Mattie and Wright, when we first arrived here.

You ask if my sewing machine came through safely! Yes — but I have not used it any yet. I made some pants for the boys out of old ones of Mr. Edgertons', but could not get any black spool thread here, so I made them "by hand." I have not had much sewing to do besides patching since I have been here. I shall make some coats for the boys before long and think I can use real silk on the machine; shall try it. I am going to send you the length of Pauline's foot, and want you to send two pairs of double-soled high shoes. Be sure and get them large enough and get good ones; a pair of calfskin and one of morocco.

Now this next that I write don't read out-loud to anyone. (If you should send any crockery, don't forget chamber furniture. All that we have is one tin wash dish and a tin chamber to match that we bought in Omaha. We can't get them here. Mr. Edgerton said that if he could find any way to send them to us he would buy them in Salt Lake and send to us. You can ask him if he did so.) My assortment of crockery of any kind is not very large, but I get along very well.

Henry received a letter from his mother last week and her likeness. He is doing very well now, and there is a prospect of his getting into a good business as soon as spring opens.

In some of my letters did I write about something for a worsted garabaldi waist for Mattie? Get something pretty and bright that will wear. I suppose that some of the folks in T. are making sugar now. I would like to help stir off some, think I would not refuse to eat some. I wonder if you can make out to read this last page? I am ashamed of it. It is written so poorly, but can't very easily remedy it now.

Remember me to all inquiring friends. . . . Love to all. From,

Mary

East Bannack
March 7th, 1864

Dear Sister,

The children have gone to bed, and Lucia and Mattie are "invited out" so I am here alone. I have been writing to Mr. Edgerton, and thought I would commence a letter to you.

I have been washing today and feel rather tired tonight. I have wished a great many times since I have been here that I could have "composition" to use when I am washing. I think the clothes would look a great deal better and I know they would wash much easier, but we cannot get the soda and lime here.

How are you all? What have you been doing today? What do you think of Mr. Edgerton's description of this country, for I presume you have seen him before this. Do you think he tells large "yarns?" If you do, just come out here and judge for yourself. It is a great country. There are two things that it abounds in, hills or mountains and sage bushes. I do really hope that some of the "folks at home," will come back with Mr. E. Am I wild in thinking of such a thing?

Henry expects to start for Salt Lake next Thursday [and] will probably be gone four or five weeks. He is going for the express company. By the way, has Mary received those gloves sent by him, by mail two weeks ago? I hope they will go through safely, for I think they are very handsome.

In my last letter to Mother I wrote that I had sowed some flower seeds in a box. Well, they are coming up. I hope they will be able to make a "live of it." I shall do all that I can to make them grow. From the way the wind blows tonight, I am afraid I shall not be able to put them into the ground for some time yet.

I have not heard from Mr. Edgerton yet, and hardly expect to before he gets back that is, if he comes as soon as he thought he should when he left here. I heard from Wilbur's folks a day or two ago. They are all well. I expect Wilbur here some time this week.

Wednesday eve. I have been baking today — have baked five loaves of bread and six pies and one platter of biscuits, and of bread pudding, made without milk, and it has taken me all day to bake them in my little stove. If I ever have a brick oven again, I shall prize it. Henry is going to bring me some butter, eggs, and sugar and perhaps some other things when he comes back from Salt Lake. Sugar is a dollar a pound and scarce at that. We expect to stay alone while he is gone.

We are all well. When that U.S. Mail gets in, that we have been looking for for the last three weeks, I shall expect to get a number of letters from home. . . . Don't forget to "write often." Love from all to all.

Mary

P.S. March 12; have just received a letter from Mr. E. written Feb. 4th.

[This letter has no date, but apparently follows that of March 7.]

Martha,

I have been writing to Mr. Edgerton and Lucy Ann and have but a few minutes more to write a few lines to you. I am sending for down to trim a hood. I think I did not say anything about lining. [I] expect to make the hood of my plaid bonnet. [I] think blue will be as pretty as any color for lining, but you may send enough of each, pink and blue silk, to line it, then I can use either. You may think it strange that I send for something every time I write, but I did not keep a copy of the list of things I sent to you, so I do not remember all that I had sent for. When I think of anything I want and am not certain that I have sent for it, I write for it. By the time this has gone I shall think of something else that I want.

Hattie and Wilbur have moved to Virginia City. Hattie and the children did not go when Wilbur did, for their goods did not go down as soon as they expected. They stayed with us two days. All are well. Hattie has been perfectly contented here, and presume she will be in her new home. . . .

I presume Mr. E. will get to Tallmadge sometime this week. Hope that he will have a "good time." I hope that his journey will not make him sick. If it should you must take care of him. How I would like to visit with him. There would be some talking done I can assure you.[5]

I dream of seeing you often. Mattie has commenced a letter to Mother but I do not think she will finish it to send this time but will send it by the next mail. Does Mary Thomas "she that was" live in T.[6] If she does, give my love to her. I intended to have written to her long ago, but have so little time that I have not written to anyone but the "folks at home." But I have not forgotten her. Henry received a letter from his grandfather last week. It is the first that he had had since he has been here.

Love from all to all, particularly to Mother. Write every week to

Mary

East Bannack
March 19, 1864

Dear Sister Martha,

The U.S. mail came in today and brought letters from home. There were none for me in particular, but I was "just as glad" as if they had all been for me. Lucia received letters from you and Belle. She says that she will answer and send in this mail which goes out Monday or the one next Monday week. Your letters were dated Jan. 19th, just two months ago.

I have sent a letter to some of you in every express that has left here since Mr. Edgerton went away. In the only letter that I have had from Mr. E. he wrote that he got everything wet in his satchel. I wonder if the letters were so that they could be read? I hope that you could read them for some of them were very impor-

[5] Edgerton arrived in Tallmadge on February 23 and left for Washington on February 25. *Summit County Beacon*, February 25 and March 3, 1864.

[6] Mary Thomas was a girl who worked for Mrs. Edgerton in Ohio.

tant. I wonder if the flower seeds I sent you were so wet as to spoil them?

I shall not write to Mr. Edgerton this mail for if he starts for home as soon as he expected to when he left here, he would not get the letter if I should write one. I wish he would <u>telegraph</u> to Salt Lake when he starts for this place. I should probably get the dispatch sometime before he would get here. Lucia has been almost sick with a cold, but is about well now. We have been having beautiful weather for a week past. It has been so warm that we have needed but very little fire and only [at] nights and mornings.

I think that "Santa Claus" was very liberal with you. He made you very nice presents. I think you will value your window shades very much. In your letter you ask if we have "meetings?" We have had one "service" in the day (Sundays) or evenings most of the time since the first of January. I do not know how long they will be kept up. The man who has preached to us expects to leave here before long. I believe it, and there is no one here to take his place.

Sunday. I have not heard from Wilbur's folks since I wrote you last, but presume they are all well or I should have heard of it. We are all very well and have got along very well since Mr. E. went away, but the time <u>seems very long since he left</u> here. I hope that he will get back before long.

People have commenced coming in here already. Over thirty came last week, who have spent the winter in Salt Lake. They say that there are a great many more on the way here and we hear from other sources that there are a great many who are expecting to come here this spring. They are all anxious to get "claims." Some of the "quartz lodes" that have been discovered since Mr. Edgerton left here are thought to be very rich. There has been a good deal of excitement over one, the "St. Paul," during the past week. It is in sight of our house. This will not be very interesting to you, but I hear so much about it and Mr. E. has what is thought to be one of the best claims on the "lode," so I feel somewhat interested in the matter.

I wish it did not take letters so long to go and come as it does. I want to hear from you every week. Write as often as you can. Henry just brought a "Beacon" to us. It looks like home. . . .

Give my best love to Mother. Tell her that Lucia will give her directions about her "trunk" when she writes. Love to all the brothers and sisters including yourself.

Mary

East Bannack
March 27, 1864

Dear Sister,

We have just received a package of letters from Lewiston. Among them were two letters from you to me, one dated July 12, the other October 5, '63. I was glad to get them if they were <u>not</u> of late date. I think we must have received <u>most</u> if not all, the letters that you have written.

In the package were letters for Lucia, Mattie, Henry, Wilbur, and Hattie. We have been looking for the Salt Lake express all day. When it comes we expect letters of later date. I hope that I shall hear from Mr. Edgerton. You don't know how long the time has seemed since he went away. I have not heard from [him] but once. I wish he was here now, for I need his advice about many things.

We are all pretty well. Lucia has not quite got over her cold, but is much better. During the last week, Lucia and I have been making over dresses for Mattie and Pauline. I made that brown dress of mine like the one Mrs. Gardner had, for Mattie. It looks very well. She has worn out and outgrown almost every dress that she had. This is a great country for wearing out clothes, particularly if they are not very strong.

Monday eve. I am too tired to write much tonight, for I have been washing today, but Henry says he thinks the express will go out tomorrow, so I will have to finish my letter tonight.

I have not much to write about that would interest you, even if I felt like writing. Sidney has some cold, the rest of the children are very well. You would be surprised to see what a great girl Mattie is. She is so large that everybody thinks she must be seventeen or eighteen years old. Henry did not go to Salt Lake two weeks ago as he expected, for he could not get anyone to take his place. He now expects "for sure" to go sometime this week. When-

83

ever he does, he will be gone five or six weeks, for he is going to bring in freight.

The weather has been some colder for a few days past, but today it is warmer again. The "miners" here are all waiting anxiously for warm weather to come, so that they can wash the dirt they have got out during the winter. Some have already washed the dirt. From the claim that Mr. Edgerton "shook" that pan of dirt last fall, the men washed fifteen hundred dollars in one day, a thousand dollars another day, and six hundred dollars another day, but that is all the good the money will do them, for as soon as they get any, they gamble and drink it all up.

Tuesday noon. Henry said the express will go out at nine o'clock so I will not have time to write but a few lines. Sidney is much better. I was afraid last night that he would have croup but he did not. Wright says "tell Homer that I have commenced a letter to him but have not finished it."

Pauline says that she would give a good deal to see Grandma and Alla and Fanny. She talks about them very often. Sidney thinks if Howard and Charlie were here he should have such fun. They could go up on the mountain and roll stones, or rocks, as the boys say here. I must not write any longer for my letter must be ready. Remember me to all the folks at home. Write often. Love to Mother,

Mary

East Bannack
April 27, 1864

Dear Sister,

I received your and Mr. Shaw's letter dated March 23, last Monday. It was very welcome, I can assure you, but it came too late to have an answer sent in this week's mail.

I am afraid that you are putting yourself to too much trouble in getting things ready to send to us. I had not thought of your going to work to dry fruit for us, but thought that some of you at home might know where you could buy some and would probably get better ones than Mr. Edgerton would. I shall value them all the more knowing that you dried them, but I am sorry that you should have to do so much extra work.

I have not felt very well for two weeks past, and have had to give up most of the housework to Lucia and Mattie. I was very much disappointed not to hear from Mr. Edgerton last mail, but hope that the reason was that he is on his way home. I shall look for him every week until he comes, and hope that I shall not have to look very long. In your letter you spoke of having very bad traveling. Here the roads have been perfectly smooth all winter and most of the time dusty. We have not had any mud. . . .

Saturday. It is the last day of April I believe. How the time does pass. It will soon be a year since we left home or rather Tallmadge, for this is our home for the present. The winter has seemed very short, and still, it seems a long time since we first came here, but we have had very little real winter weather, compared to our Ohio winters.

I like the climate here very much. You write that it does not seem near as far to Idaho since Mr. E. has visited you, as it did before. I was very sure that you would all feel so, and am glad that you do. We shall look for letters from home again tomorrow — for it is the day for the mail to arrive from Salt Lake — and I shall be just foolish enough to look for Mr. Edgerton. I shall not feel very much disappointed if he does not come for I have no reason to expect him but think it barely possible that he may come. When he does, I shall have a thousand questions to ask about you all. I hope that he will remember all that is said to him, so he can tell us every little thing. [It] will be of interest to us. . . .

In Mr. Shaw's letter he speaks of Martha's children going to your house to visit and says that they generally go down [the] cellar and help themselves to apples. Wouldn't my children like to do the same thing? They have talked a great deal about apples this winter and have had three or four to eat. Now they think they would like to be where they could have maple sugar and molasses to eat. I would not refuse to eat either if I could have some just as well as not.

Tell Mr. Shaw that some of us will answer his letter and send with this if we can get the time before the mail goes out. When I write I intend the letter for both of you, but address it to you for it seems more natural that I should do so. It is not because I do not want to hear <u>from him for I am always glad to get his letters</u>. Lucia has commenced a letter to Mr. Shaw but will not have time to finish it before this mail goes out.

Sunday eve. Henry has just got back from Salt Lake. Have not seen him. Write to us soon if it does not hurt your eyes too much. Give my love to the brothers and sisters and keep a good share for herself. Give my best love to Mother. I hope she has entirely recovered from her sickness. Tell her that I would like her here very much, this spring particularly.

Mary

East Bannack
May 22nd, 1864

Dear Sister,

I received your letter dated April 25th today. I was very glad to get it and still I was disappointed too, for it did not give any encouragement of Mr. Edgerton's coming home very soon.

I was <u>very much</u> disappointed because he did not come <u>today</u>. I was so <u>sure</u> that he would come, because we did not get a letter from any of you last week. I do not know what Mr. E. will think because I have not written more to him — but I thought that if he should start for home, as soon as he expected, when he left here, he would not get my letters if I should write. So I have not written for some time.[7]

I have not been very well for four or five weeks past — the rest of the family are pretty well. We have had an almost unheard of thing for this country, that is rain. During the past week we have had some very heavy showers, but the roof of our house is so well made that it did not leak until the last shower — day before yesterday; then it did not leak very badly. But if it had rained again

[7] As Mrs. Edgerton wrote this letter, her husband was still in Washington. He left that city in the first week of June and arrived in Tallmadge en route back to Montana on June 4. He left Tallmadge on June 6 (*Summit County Beacon*, June 9, 1864). The day after writing this letter, Mrs. Edgerton gave birth to her daughter Idaho.

yesterday, I do not know [but that] we should have been as badly served as some of our neighbors. [We] would have been "[?]," that is, have the roof all washed off, and everything wet with <u>mud</u>. I hope it won't rain again for six months.

In your letter you sent a list of the things that you have sent in a box by Charlie Sackett.ˣ I can make good use of everything you have sent and I am <u>very very</u> thankful for them. I shall think a great deal of the current jelly, for it [is] something we can't get here and the dried corn too. Well! I can't tell what I shall think the most of — shall think a great deal of all of it. I hope that I shall be able sometime to repay <u>you all</u> for your kindness, but do not know how I can do so.

You wrote that some thought that the peaches had been killed by the severe cold weather. I hope that is not true, for you will all miss them so much. How is it with the other fruit, apples, grapes, &c.? Are they injured any?

You spoke of "independent comp[any]" "reporting themselves ready for duty." Does Homer belong to the comp.? I think that he wrote to Mattie that he was a "Drummer boy?" Will he go with them into camp? I received a letter from Hattie last week. She wrote that the children were never healthier than they are now. She was well but Wilbur had not been very well for a few days. I expect him here sometime this week . (I wish I could say the same of Mr. E.) Henry had not been here but a few days during the past five or six weeks since he came back from Salt Lake. He has been to Virginia twice and is now between here and Salt Lake on business for the express co. I don't know how long he will be gone. He was very well when he was here last.

Pauline wants me to tell Alla that she has got another little black and white kitty, She calls it "Spotty." I believe it was given to Mattie but she (P.) calls it hers. I meant to have answered that letter from your boys to our children before this — will try to answer it before long. Give my love to Mother and the rest of the friends. All send love.

Mary

ˣ Charles Sackett was a friend from Ohio who came to Montana with Richard Fenn in mid-1864.

Bannack
May 29, 1864[9]

Dear Mother,

While the rest are eating supper I will add a few lines to Mattie's letter. I am getting along very well but I miss Mother's kind care and advice. It seems as if I was really alone. I don't know what I should do if it were not for Lucia. She is worth her weight in gold. It worries me to think that she has so much to do but it is impossible to get anyone to help about anything but washing and pretty hard to hire anyone to do that. I don't know as you will be able to read this. Please excuse all mistakes. Love to all in haste.

Mary

East Bannack
June 4, 1864

Dear Sister,

I received your letter of May 3rd just one month after date. How strange it is that you don't hear anything from Mr. Edgerton. Do you suppose that he is sick?

I have not heard a word from him for a number of weeks past and I am afraid that he is sick. I shall be glad when he gets back again — the days have seemed very long since the baby was born. If I was able to be around at work, the time would not seem as long.

I am getting along very well, have been out to eat supper with the rest of the family twice. The baby is very quiet — have not had to be awake nights with her at all. She is not only a good baby, but they all say that she is pretty.

Lucia and Mattie attended a wedding last week, May 25. Mattie can give Mary a description of the performance at the wedding — but I doubt if anyone can give a description of the "chivaree" that they had about eleven o'clock. It was before the

---

[9] This note is written at the bottom of a letter from Mattie Edgerton to Lucy Foster Wright, May 29, 1864 (Edgerton Family Papers, MHS). In her letter, Mattie noted that her mother was " 'as well as could be expected,' has been up two or three times. The baby looks prettier every day. It was weighed yesterday and weighs just nine pounds."

girls came home. I knew that the couple were to be chivareed, but after all it startled me so that I did not get over it for some time. I did not sleep very well that night. The next night we had a <u>regular serenade</u> and it was really very fine. That did not disturb me, I slept better after hearing it. Lucia and Mattie have been to call on the bride this afternoon and have just got back. They found some beautiful flowers by the side of the road. I will send you a few specimens. The "Bee Larkspur" grows wild here. They do not grow quite as large as when cultivated — I never prized flowers as much as I do this spring. I don't [know] but it is because I did not think we should have any here. But since the rain all sorts of beauties have sprung up in unlooked places. I will try and save seed of some of the handsomest ones. I wish <u>I</u> was able to go after flowers so that I could tell by the leaf of the plant where to gather seed.

Sunday afternoon. I received letters this morning from you and Lucy Ann mailed May 6th. You wonder that we don't get your letters sooner? We have lately got them in about a month after they were written. There was a time that the mails were very irregular because of the deep snow between this place and Salt Lake, but they are very regular now and we often have two or three extra mail coaches and expresses come in during the week loaded with passengers. I must not write much more for my arm aches. I am not very strong yet. Tell Lucy Ann that I will write to her the next letter. [I] would write today if I was not so tired. Love to all from all.

Mary

East Bannack
July 13

Dear Sister,

I received your letter dated June 19th today and will answer it today if I have time.

Mr. Edgerton arrived here July 1. He finally took us all by surprise. We had been looking all day for him and supposed that he would come in a coach, but the coach went directly to Virginia and left him and his trunk at the junction sixty miles from here.

He was obliged to buy a horse, saddle and bridle to come here with. [He] left his trunk at the junction and it is there yet. He got here about six o'clock at night, tired enough. I need not say that we were all glad to see him.

Hattie and Wilbur and Jimmie came here last week Thursday and stayed until yesterday morning. You can image that <u>we did some talking</u> while she was here. We were all much disappointed because the trunk had not come. The express co. has sent for it and it ought to have been here before this. Mr. Edgerton <u>did not</u> take the letters from the trunk that he left at Atchison, for he did not think that they were in it. We shall probably get them sometime in September.

We had a celebration here on the Fourth. It was got up on short notice. Speeches were made by Mr. Edgerton and two others. The howitzer was fired in front of our house fully as many times as we wanted to hear it. Wright and Sidney ran their flag up on our house, and fired their little lead cannon in the place of firecrackers.

Mr. Edgerton received a letter today from Charlie Sackett mailed at Ft. Laramie June 25th. He says that they have got along so far very well and expect to get here about the first of August.

Mr. Edgerton, Wilbur, Mr. Thompson and a number of others are expecting to go next week about forty miles from here on a fishing excursion to catch salmon. If Hattie comes here with Wilbur, she and Lucia and perhaps Mattie will go with them. They will probably be gone three days. . . .

We are all well — the baby grows finely — and is a very good baby.

Sister Martha, Mary has given me permission to write a few lines, on condition I would write about the baby. Well, it is a wonderful child, weighs twelve pounds and a half, has blue eyes, is <u>white</u> and is said to be good-looking. We call it Lucia Idaho, which being interpreted signifies <u>the light and gem of the mountains</u>. There is a name for you, and you called it "a what is it." Great excitement here about newly discovered silver mines about 12 miles from here. Love to all with the respect of my youngest daughter.

S. Edgerton

East Bannack
July 31, 1864

Dear Sister Martha,

We received yours of the 10th today. [I] was glad to hear from you and [to] hear that you were all well. . . .

We are all well. Mr. Edgerton has gone, with Wilbur and others, to Deer Lodge about one hundred miles from here on a fishing excursion. They expected to be gone a week.

We had a few days of very warm weather during the past week, but there is one comfort, the nights are cool and pleasant. "That" trunk came last week, all safe. I like my bonnet very much and all the rest of the "things." I hardly know how to thank you all, for the many presents that you sent us. You ask how my dresses fit? They are rather large and long for me, but I can remedy that very easily. I like them very much. The "girls" hats are the oddest-looking hats I ever saw. I presume you wrote how to trim them, but the letters are back in that other trunk. We shall look for Charlie Sackett and Richard Fenn in a few days. There are three letters from Tallmadge here waiting for Charlie. Henry received a letter from his mother today — was much surprised to learn that she is in Tallmadge. He has not had a letter from his grandfather for a long time.

Henry has improved very much both in "looks and appearance" since he came here. He is a steady good boy. We have a new minister here now — he is a graduate of Auburn Seminary, by the name of Smith. I don't know whether it is John Smith or not. He says that he knew Mr. and Mrs. Seyur there. I am not much acquainted with him yet, but he appears like a very pleasant man.

Monday. The mail goes out at four o'clock this afternoon. Lucia and I have finished our washing and if the baby is quiet I will finish this letter to send tonight. We are to have mail three times a week now. You wrote that Junius was going to work in Akron. I suppose by that he has decided not to come here. I would like to see him. Mr. Edgerton has been looking for him, for he thought he was coming here sometime this summer. . . .

Mr. Edgerton's "commission" making him Governor of Montana came yesterday. None of the officers that have been appointed have come here yet. I don't know where the capital will be yet. I must send this letter to the office now or it will be too late. I will try to write again this week, but my time is pretty well taken up with housework and baby tending. All send love to you all. Pauline says lots of love to Grandma and Alla. Give my best to Patty — I wish I could see her.

Your description of your visit at Mr. Smith's seems like old times. I never knew a family so thoroughly selfish as that family. I should not trouble them very much if I was there. I can tell you it makes me provoked every time I think of them. In haste,

Mary

Aug. 3, 1864

I did not get my letter finished in time for the mail Monday for it went out earlier than usual, so I will write a few lines and send today. . . .

Mr. Edgerton has got back from his fishing excursion. He brought home enough fish (speckled trout) to last us a long time. He now expects to go to Virginia next week and wants me to go with him. I don't know whether I shall or not. I think it will be a hard ride for the baby. Lucia is going over there to spend a week before long.

Tell Mother that the shawl she sent me is a beauty. I thank her very much for it, and thank you for the table spread. It is so nice that I am almost afraid to use it. I like all the dress goods very much, particularly the merino. Pauline's "dolly" is the admiration of all the children around here. I do not let her have it every day for fear she will break it. I shall not have the time to answer the childrens' letter today, but will before long. I would like very much to visit with Patty while she is with you. I have not time to write more. I wish you all could see my baby. She is what they say around here "real pert." We all think she is a wonderful baby.

Mary

92

Bannack

September 11, 1864

Dear Sister,

When I wrote last to Martha I <u>really</u> intended to have written to you the next week. But Lucia did not get back from Virginia until the last of the week and then she was so near sick that she did not feel able to do much, so I did not get much time to write. Since then the Indians have troubled the "stage line" so much that they are stopped carrying the mail any farther than Denver, so I have put off writing.[10] It is possible that <u>this</u> letter may go to the states by California. If it does not, I don't know how soon you will get it. I have not heard from Tal. For a number of weeks and I miss the letters very much.

Mr. Sackett and Mr. Fenn have been <u>here</u> two weeks. They arrived in Virginia Aug. 11th. They are building themselves a cabin, will finish it this week I think. It really seems good to have them so near us. The box that they brought for us came pretty nearly all right. One or two cans of jelly leaked down and made some of the things rather sticky, but did not injure anything.

Tuesday morn. This paper was clean when I commenced writing but it has accidently got badly soiled. I hope you will excuse it. Tell Clem that when we opened that box we found a number of short letters from him. One was written on the churn. Lucia thinks it will be her own fault if she does not make good butter after getting those directions. We found other letters in the pails of tea. By the way, that tea is excellent. We have tried the dried apples and the dried corn and found both <u>good</u>. Most of the apples that we get here are very tasteless. I like <u>these</u> because they are sour.

We are all well. The weather is quite cool now, so that a fire mornings and evenings seems very acceptable. It snowed on the

---

[10] By the early 1860s, the Indians of the Far West were becoming increasingly alarmed at the white migration into their territories, and during the Civil War, resistance broke out both in the Northwest and in the Southwest. In 1864, the principal Indian difficulty was in Colorado, and culminated in the Sand Creek Massacre of November 29, 1864. In addition, in that year the Sioux Indians of the northern plains became restive and fought a number of inconclusive engagements with federal troops. The Montana settlements were never in real danger of Indian attack during this period, but travel and communications to and from Montana were sometimes interrupted as a result of the Indian difficulties.

mountains near us Sunday morning. Since I wrote to Martha there have been some very fine <u>silver lodes</u> discovered near here. New discoveries both of gold and silver are being made every week and almost every day. Last week there was a sale made on the Dacotah Lode. A New York company bought one claim (no. 6) one hundred feet and quartz mill with it, and paid fifty-eight thousand dollars in coin for it. Those specimens that Mr. Edgerton had last winter were taken from that claim. Mr. Edgerton owned one-fourth of Claim No. 4 on the same Lode.

We heard last mail that Atlanta was taken. It is good news. I hope that we shall soon hear that Richmond is taken. I wish that we could get the papers from the States, we should have a "fuller" account of our victory. All the news we get now is telegraphic.[11]

I don't know that you will be able to read all of this for I have been writing and rocking the baby at the same time. Mr. Edgerton has just brought me a <u>peach</u>. We can buy <u>three</u> for one dollar. Don't [you] think they are cheap? We had a present last week of some potatoes and turnips that were raised near Virginia. We measured one of the turnips and it measures $21\frac{1}{4}$ inches in circumference! The other turnips were nearly as large. We can buy potatoes now for ten cents per lb. Tell Mr. Shaw that Mr. Edgerton will answer his letter before long. Love to all.

Mary

Tell Martha that I was weighed a few days ago. I weigh 117 lbs. The baby weighs 15 lbs. I will try to write again before long to some of you at home.

Mary

[11] Mrs. Edgerton's "telegraphic news" was not as instantaneous as the term implies. Probably her reference is to the *Montana Post,* published in Virginia City. It was Montana's first newspaper and began publication August 27, 1864. Telegraph service did not reach Montana until November 3, 1866. In the meantime, the *Post* printed "telegraphic news" which it culled from other papers. Allegedly, the *Post*'s editors had an arrangement with the local postmaster to the effect that when "foreign" newspapers arrived in the mail the postmaster held up their delivery until the *Post* had first cannibalized the national news from them for its telegraphic columns. Mrs. Edgerton may also be referring to the *Union Vedette* which, until the *Post* began publication, had the largest circulation of any paper in the territory. The paper was published by Union soldiers in Salt Lake City and probably did have the benefits

Bannack
September 18th, 1864

Dear Mother,

It is a long time since I have written a letter to you, but do not think that I have forgotten you. I do not get much time to write "these days." We are now in the midst of the dirtiest kind of work. Mr. Edgerton has been taking the mud all off of both the outside and inside of our house and plastering it over with lime. It makes <u>us</u> a great deal of hard, dirty work. If we could finish <u>one</u> room and then work at another, we could get along much easier, but we are obliged to have all the rooms turned "<u>upside</u> down" if not "inside out" at the same time. I hope that we shall get straightened around again this week.

I have wished a great many times that Mary Thomas was here for I think that she would help me occasionally. There is a woman that lives near us that helps me wash sometimes and I would hire her every week but she cannot leave her family always when I want her. I pay her two and a half dollars (everything has to be paid in gold here. It would [be] twice as much in greenbacks)[12] for doing all the rubbing. We bring all the water, tend the fire and wring and hang out all the clothes. If Mary was here and was willing to do so, she could make much money, but she would have to endure many privations. Mr. Fenn and Mr. Sackett have finished their cabin, all but the floor, slept in it for the first time last night.

It is very pleasant to have them so near us. Their cabin is right opposite us with the "Grasshopper" between. We expect to stay here this winter even if the Legislature should be called to meet at some other place. I am very glad, for it is so much work to move, even if we have but little to move.

We have not heard from "that other trunk" yet. Have sent to Salt Lake for it, if it is there. We do not know but that the Indians have <u>confiscated</u> it. If they have, think what a nice time they will

of telegraphic news dispatches. Still, by the time the paper reached the Montana camps, its news could be quite dated.

12 In the western territories, far from the seat of the national government, the government's legal-tender notes, "greenbacks," circulated well below their face value. In Montana in 1864, greenbacks circulated at fifty percent of their face value.

have parading around with our corsets and hoop skirts on — saying nothing of the "lots" of other things that are in the trunk.

We have made arrangements to send to "Bitter Root" for flour and vegetables to use this winter.[13] We can get them there much cheaper than at Salt Lake. We have to pay from twenty-five to twenty-eight dollars a sack for flour now, and I don't [know] how much higher it will be before the winter is over.

We have not heard from the States for a long time. I shall be glad when the mail can go through again without any interruptions from the Indians. I will then try to be more prompt in writing home. We are all well. The baby grows finely and is the best baby that I ever had the care of. She is perfectly healthy. You would be surprised to see how much Pauline has grown since we left Tallmadge. She talks about Grandma very often. Give my love to all the "folks at home."

Mary

Bannack
Oct. 30, 1864

Dear Sister,

We have not received any letters from home since the mail commenced running again. Today's mail has not yet come in, but hope it will come before bedtime and bring us "lots" of letters from home. Mr. Sackett and Mr. Fenn have received a number of letters lately so we hear some home news. Lucia received the news of her Father's death last week. She had not heard anything of his sickness. He had been sick for sometime with chronic dysentary.

Eight o'clock. The mail has just come in but is not all distributed. Wright has a letter from Sammy and in it is one for me dated August 12th. . . .

We get *The Beacon* pretty regularly now. In the one that we got last week I see that Mr. Andrew Fenn <u>declines</u> to run for

[13] The southern end of the Bitter Root Valley was about seventy-five miles northwest of Bannack. Catholic missionaries had established a mission in the Valley in 1841 and had cultivated wheat. In 1850, the missionaries sold their improvements to one John Owen who expanded agricultural production. The Valley was well suited to this kind of activity and when gold was discovered in Montana, farmers began to work in the Valley growing crops for sale in the mining camps.

sheriff. What is the reason? We have been having a pretty warm election here. Wilbur was nominated [for] delegate to Congress on the Union ticket and a Mr. McLean on the Democratic ticket. Mr. Edgerton has not received all the returns yet, but from all we can hear [we] suppose that the Union ticket is defeated. All "Sesech" voted the Democratic ticket.[14]

I am very sorry that Wilbur is defeated for I don't like to have the party defeated. [That] is one reason. Another is Hattie could and would have made a good visit in Tallmadge this winter and that would do us all good. . . .

Tuesday. I will finish this to send out today. Wright is not feeling very well this morning, has taken cold I think. He says that he will answer Sammy's letter before long. We've had beautiful weather during the past month, until the last of the month. The ground was covered with snow two inches deep Sunday morning. It is most all gone now. We had a little snow in Sept. but it did not last long.

I walked down to Marysville[15] a mile and a half last week to see the new steam quartz mills. One has twelve stamps, the other has twenty-eight. It is quite a sight to see them. I have written you that I had received that binding for my duster but perhaps you have not got the letter. I have not made the duster over yet but will when I get the time to do it. I don't know as you can read this very readily. I am so cold that my hand trembles badly.

We all received letters, even the Baby, from Mr. Gardner, last week. Lucia will write to you when she can get time. She has a good many [two words indecipherable]. Remember us to Junius when you see him. We should be very glad to see him here. I will send you a sprig of sweet-scented grass. I don't know whether the seed is ripe or not. All send love to all.

Mary

November 1

The man has come back from Bitter Root with our potatoes, cabbages, onions, and flour. I wish you could see the potatoes. I

---

[14] See pages 56–58 for treatment of the election.

[15] Marysville was a small mining camp just downstream from Bannack.

never saw or tasted better ones. Mr. Edgerton had a box of white mershanacks sent him. (Is that the way to spell it? I don't know!) The largest one weighed three and a half pounds, the smallest three-fourths of a pound. They are very smooth. There were about a half a bushel in the box, and we had to buy them at twenty-five cents per lb. They would not cost a little.

We have had a cellar dug under our kitchen floor to keep our vegetables in. I don't know how much they will cost us yet. Will tell you in my next. I tell you the farmers are getting rich in this territory. There is demand for everything they can raise and they can raise everything here that you can raise in Ohio. I do not think that the winters will be as bad for peach trees and grape vines as they are in the states, the atmosphere is so dry here.

I have not had time to write more today, will write again Sunday if I can get time.

Mary

Lucia received a small box of apples and peaches from a man who crossed the plains with us and is now in Salt Lake. There were seven large apples and three times as many peaches weighing in all eight pounds. It was sent by express and he paid $4.50 for it.

I can tell you that apples never tasted half as good to us as they do now, but they cost too much to buy many here and we get along very well without them.

Mary

Bannack
Nov. 6th, 1864

Dear Sister,

Since I wrote you last week, [the] election news shows that Wilbur is elected to Congress so Hattie will go with him to the states and spend the winter in Tallmadge. They will start now very soon and expect to go as far as Salt Lake and perhaps farther in their own conveyance. I don't know whether they will be able to visit here before they go or not.

I have had the baby's likeness taken to send to Mother. It is not a "first rate" likeness for she did not keep very still. I did not think that I could have put a short dress that was not white on her. It could have made a much better picture. The chair that she sat in is Pauline's "little" barrel chair. Do you recognize the cover of it?

Now while I think of it, I want you to get some "Swedish turnip seed" of Mr. Hinman and send [it] here to us. I do not think that there are turnips of that kind raised here. Don't forget to do so. Another thing, if I don't forget it, I will send you some money and I want you to send some postage stamps. We cannot get them here. I don't know but I could get them in Virginia but to be sure of some I will send to you. . . .

Mr. Edgerton has finally concluded to call the "Legislature" at this place. The Virginians do not like it very well. They think it ought to be called there and it would have been if there were not so many "Copperheads" there. I am very glad that it is to meet here because Mr. Edgerton can be at home all the time.

It has been snowing most of the time today but it is not very cold. I just asked Mr. E. if he had any word to send you. He said nothing in particular. He supposed that I had "bragged" about the baby all that it was necessary, for we all think she is the greatest baby in the country. She has two teeth and two more teeth almost through.

Tell Clarinda that I hope she and Hattie will have a "good time" this winter. I don't wish that I was going to take the journey that she is going to take, but I would like to make such a visit. You must visit with her all you can while she is there and I will visit her when she comes back. Don't let Mrs. Fenn and Clarinda keep her there and let Wilbur come back alone, for we all want her here.

Henry is very well. He received letters from his Mother, sister and Grandfather last week and had one from Homer. We are all well but Pauline. She has a sore throat and is just as Wright was last week. It is nothing serious. Love to all.

Mary

Bannack
Nov. 13, 1864

Dear Mother,

Mattie is writing to some of the girls, so I thought [I] would write a few lines to you and send in the same envelope with hers. The other children are listening to Lucia who is reading her journal. They all remember most of the places where we camped and are very much interested. When I think of it, I think what a <u>long</u>, <u>long</u> way we are from you all. But if we have good success here, I hope it will not be many years before we should see you again.

When I wrote last to Martha, I supposed that Wilbur was elected delegate to Congress, but find that I was mistaken. I will not write particulars, for you will probably hear them from Hattie's letters to Clarinda. I am very sorry, for it must be a great disappointment to them both. They had rented their house and expected to have started for the states in a few days when they heard the news. I expected to have sent the baby's likeness to you by Hattie, but now I think I will send it by mail. I wish it was a better likeness but you can form some idea of her looks by it. She has a <u>little longer</u> neck than that shows, but it is not very long. I think she is the healthiest of all my babies, and she is very good looking. I would like to show her to you.

Sunday eve. I have had to stop writing to get supper, so my letter will be too late for today's mail and now I will have to wait until Tuesday before I can send it. We did not get any mail from the States today, have not had any for two weeks. I hope that the Indians have not interfered with the mail again. It does not [seem] to me that we are so far from you all when we can hear from there often.

I had a woman to sew for me last week. She fitted four and made the waists of three dresses for Lucia and Mattie, but tell Louise that her (the woman) sewing did not look much like Louise's. But it is <u>so much</u> done and we can remedy some of it. She had a child here with her and of course could not do as much as she could have done without it. I paid her seven dollars. I have sold a number of those largest pans that were sent in that box for one dollar each and sold one of the largest pails for $1.50. It was bruised some.

I opened the pail of lard last week and found it as sweet as new lard. We had a few days of very cold weather and since then it has been mild and pleasant. Henry is drawing wood from the mountains, now. [He] is very well. The legislature will meet here on the 12th of Dec. The secretary of the Territory is not here yet. Mr. Edgerton has telegraphed to the president about it, and asked to have another secretary appointed, but has not received an answer yet.

I suppose you have thanksgiving next week. Wish we could be with you. I don't know whether we shall have a Thanksgiving supper or not. We are all well. . . . I let Lucia have that green merino for a dress for I do not need one this winter. That trunk has not come yet.

Tuesday. I have not time to get that likeness ready to send today, but it is yours when it does come. Much love to you all, especially from

Mary

Bannack
Sunday eve.
Nov. 20, 1864

Dear Sister,

Lucia is writing to you, so I have given the baby to Mattie to hold a while so I can write a few lines to you too. We received your letter dated Oct. 18th today. I am sorry to hear that Mother is lame — hope she has got over it before this.

I have thought a great deal about her this fall. I hope she will be spared to us for many years yet. . . .

You ask if I have made my hood yet? No, for I have not had the time to make it yet. That <u>trunk</u> has not got here yet, but we look every day for it. It ought to have been here two weeks ago, for it has been nearly six weeks since it left Salt Lake. We need some of the things that are in it very much.

The boys have <u>outgrown</u> the coats that I made for them last spring, so I will have to make other ones as soon as I get the cloth. Mr. Edgerton's clothes are all in that trunk. His wrappers and drawers would be very acceptable now.

The "people here" are building an office for Mr. Edgerton (The Governor) joining our house. I think it will be a very "good looking" building for this place. This "City" has improved very much during the last two months.

Monday eve. We have done our washing today, had supper, and Lucia has gone to her "german" lessons. Mr. Edgerton has gone up town and if no one comes in I will try to finish this tonight. I don't know how we shall manage to send out letters for we are nearly out of postage stamps, and the P.M. will not send them without.

Our minister is going to preach a thanksgiving sermon next Thursday. I would like to get up a supper that day if you could all be here. It would seem like Thanksgiving then. Mr. Edgerton is very busy now, getting buildings ready for the legislature. It is the secretary's business to see to all those things, but he is not here, and the legislature meets here in three weeks. It will take some time to get the buildings ready and the furniture made. I do not think the room will be fitted up quite in the "style" that they are in Washington.

You wrote about the school. I wish our children could be in school this winter. They study some every day at home but it is not like being in school. I should hardly like to send them to school here, if there was one, for they would learn so many bad things that would injure them more than all the good they would learn. Most of the boys here swear as soon as they can talk. Our boys have not got any of those habits yet and I hope they will not.

Well! Lucia has got home and is jabbering in dutch so that it puts me out. I suspect that when we go back to "America" she will be a regular dutchman. I think I will have to write to you as Willie Fenn did to Wright that it will take two lawyers to read this page of my letter. I think every time I write a letter that the next time I will take more time but I do not do it, for I have to write when the baby is asleep or when someone is holding her. We received that letter from Frederich — tell Clem that Lucia is going to answer for herself whether she can make butter out of water or not, so I will not say anything about it. Love to all, from

Mary

Bannack
Nov. 27, 1864

Dear Sister,

We did not get any letters from home today, but I will answer the ones that <u>ought</u> to have come. I may not give just such answers as the letter requires but will try my best.

I have not been well for a few days past but feel much better today. I have not been so sick but that I have been up and around all the time. I took cold on Thanksgiving Day. We got up a supper that day on short notice. Had Mr. Sackett and Fenn and seven other gentlemen here for supper. They all seemed to enjoy it very much. I kept thinking of you all, and wondering where you met to eat your thanksgiving supper, and who were there? Did you have baked "<u>Mountain Sheep</u>" (it is excellent) for supper? We did, and had baked chicken instead of turkey. Last week we had given us some moose meat and a quarter of mountain sheep weighing over thirty pounds, and about six pounds of fresh pork.[16] This last you may not think a great rarity, but it <u>is</u> here. We bought some two weeks ago and it was the first I had tasted since I left Tallmadge.

Mr. Edgerton has just commenced writing his <u>message</u>. He has to write nights because there are so many interruptions during the day. He has to "<u>oversee</u>" the building of the houses for the legislature to meet in because the Secretary is not here.

Sunday, Dec. 4th. I commenced this a week ago and thought I should finish it Tuesday, but Hattie and her children came here on Monday night (and are here yet; will stay part of this week) so I have not had time to write. I have just finished the boys' shirts and expect to make Wright a coat and pants this week for I don't know [but] what he will be hired as <u>page</u> for one of the "<u>houses</u>" while they are in session, and if he is hired he must be all ready a week from tomorrow.

Oh! Our trunk came when Hattie did. The lock was broken but I don't know whether anything was taken out or not for I don't

[16] This is the first in a series of gifts that Mrs. Edgerton mentions, and the gift-giving will continue until the legislature adjourns. When the legislators and lobbyists left town, the stream of gifts dried up.

know what was in it. But [of] the articles that were on the bill that was sent last summer, I have not received any three bottles of glycerin or six bottles magnetic ointment or candle wick. I supposed they were all in that trunk. I have been waiting for the wick to make candles, but it is not there, and there were eight yards of binding for the boys' coats on the bill, but there is none in the trunk, and no buttons for their coats. I don't know how many yards of cambric were sent. There are twelve yards on the bill — there was none in this trunk and only enough for the dresses in the other trunk.

Sunday, December 11. I think that I am very smart when it takes me three weeks to write one letter. I should have finished this letter before if I could have mailed it, but the roads are so blocked up with snow, that mails are very irregular now. Hattie is here yet, expects to go home Tuesday if it is not too cold. We have had very cold weather during the last week, much milder tonight. We have more snow this winter than last, but not as much as in Virginia [City]. We are all well. The children grow so fast that I can hardly keep them in clothes. I have made one pair of pants for Wright; expect to begin his coat tomorrow.

The "Members" have come and the legislature will meet tomorrow.[17] There are so many talking that I make all sorts of mistakes. When our office is done I will try to get a "picture" of our premesis and send [it to] you. And if I can get pictures of the mountains near us will send them. They look finely now covered with snow.

Hattie is writing to Clarinda, Mattie to Mary, and Lucia is writing German. We've all enjoyed Hattie's visit here very much. I wish she lived here. Wilbur is building a new house in Virginia and expected to have it finished before this, but it has been too cold to work at it. I don't know whether I wrote you that Henry has bought a span of mules and is drawing wood from the mountains. He is doing <u>well</u>. I am "saving in" all the "specimens" of gold and silver ore that I can get. Shall keep them to take back to the States some day. I have some very handsome ones. I will try to write again next mail.

[17] See pages 57–59 for details of the legislative session.

I had a beautiful present today from Mr. Gridley, a pin made of native gold. It cost twenty-five dollars in gold. I wish you could see it. We all went uptown and were weighed last week. Hattie [weighs] 115, Lucia 138, and I weigh 102 pounds. "Ain't" I heavy? Love to all,

Mary

Bannack
Dec. 18th, 1864

Dear Sister,

We received a letter yesterday from Wilbur saying that Junius was on his way here, and had letters for us. That accounts for our not getting letters very lately by mail. I am very glad that Junius is coming here for I think he can do well here. I received a letter from Abbie last week. It is the only one since I left Tallmadge.

I forgot to write in my last that Mr. Edgerton brought back a nightshirt that did not belong to him. I presume it is one that you lent him and he put it in his trunk thinking it was his. We are all well. I am beginning to grow fat again, think I shall weigh as much as you do by next spring.

The "Legislature" and the "Governor" have had quite a time of it the last week. Some of the members did not like to take the "oath" prescribed by Congress, but finally they all took it but one member. He has been a commissioned officer in the rebel (Price's) army, but he was admitted to his seat, and then a committee was appointed to tell Mr. Edgerton that they were ready to hear any communication from him. He sent back word that when they were organized according to the law passed by Congress he would communicate with them, and not before. The next day Rogers (the rebel) resigned. I will send you the papers giving an account of it if I can keep them long enough! There are so few taken here that they are used up pretty fast.

We are having steady cold weather now. [The] snow [is] about three inches deep here, but on the mountains it is very deep. On the Divide, about seventy-five miles between here and Salt Lake, many cattle have been snowed in and frozen to death. It is not as cold now. There is much more snow in the mountains now than there was last winter. . . .

Wright is much pleased with his situation as page, for he feels that he is learning something.[18] He will get three or four dollars a day. He is a good deal like Homer about that. He and Sidney have the reputation of being the best boys in town. Perhaps I have written the same before. If I have you need not read this.

In the letter I sent last week I wrote you about the contents of that second trunk. Did you get the letter? I don't know whether you get all of my letters or not. I have not written every week for I could not get time. We do not have mail now only once a week. Tell Lucy Ann that I have not received that letter that you said she had written.

We shall look for Junius every coach now until he comes. I hope he will get through safely. It must be very cold riding, but the coach is full every time that it leaves here, of men going back to the states expecting to return here again in the spring.

Oh! I forgot to write to you about those picture cards that you sent. I have not shown them to any of the children. I thought I would keep them until Christmas. I would like to spend Christmas and New Years with you. The mail will not go out until Tuesday. If I have time I will write some tomorrow.

Mary

I have got through washing and it is time to get supper so I cannot write any more this time. I wrote you some time ago to send me some Swedish turnip seeds. Did you get the letter? I would like some tomato seeds too, if you have any to spare.

It has seemed very lonely since Hattie went home. I wish she lived here. Tell Mother that I am afraid to send that ambrotype of the baby by mail for fear that it will get broken. I think that I will have a chance to send it by someone going to the states. All send love to you all.

Mary

[18] Both of the Edgerton sons worked as pages for the first legislature, Wright in the Council and Sidney in the House.

Chapter 5

The Letters of Mary Edgerton, 1865

Bannack
Jan. 2nd, 1865

Dear Sister,

I HAVE BEEN writing to Abbie and it [is] almost time for the mail to close, but I will write a few lines to you and send with Mattie's to let you know that we are all well. I have not sent any letter home for two weeks and didn't know but that you would think that I was sick. But I am not — am very well and so are all the rest of us.

I have just got through washing and it is almost time to get supper. Perhaps you would <u>like</u> to know what I am going to have for supper? Well! Last Saturday we had a present of a hind quarter of antelope. I am going to fry some of that and bake potatoes and soda biscuit. Those are the substantials; for desert, mince pie. I cannot get up a very great variety for want of the materials to do it with.

I kept those "flower pictures" that were in that trunk for the childrens' Christmas presents. They were <u>very much</u> pleased with them. I think they are perfect beauties. Mr. Edgerton bought three apples for the younger children, paid two dollars in greenbacks for them. Junius did not get here last week; shall certainly expect him this week. We have mail now only once a week. Shall expect a letter every mail. I would like to write a longer letter, but must stop and get supper. Love to all.

Mary

Bannack City
Jan. 15th, 1865

Dear Mother,

I did not get any letter from home last week but suppose that there is one on the way for me. I do not know whether Junius has arrived in Virginia or not. We have been expecting Wilbur here for a number of days past to attend court which is now in session.

I presume that he finds it more work to get moved and settled in his new house than he thought it would be. I think Hattie will be glad when they get in their new house for they have been living with another family ever since they got ready to go to the States. They expected that their house would have been finished before Christmas but the weather was so cold that the men could not work on it.

The legislature is still in session. Mr. Edgerton sent the only printed copy of his message that we had to Clem. Will send one to you as soon as it is printed in pamphlet form. The "boys" think they are earning a good deal now that the bill has passed giving them each five dollars a day. They hardly know what they shall do with the money when they get it. I tell them that we can find ways enough to use the money when flour is twenty-eight dollars a sack and sugar is one dollar a pound. When everything is so high, it seems as if I wanted to use twice as much as I do at any other time.

I have just used the last of that pail of lard that came in that box. It was just as fresh and sweet as new lard. I wish I had as much more. We can get lard here but it is not always fresh and then it costs a good deal. I don't know the present price but presume it is one dollar a pound. We pay $1.75 per lb. for "fresh ranch butter" and it is scarce at that price.

Monday afternoon. I stopped writing last eve. to go to church and when I got home [I] had to tend "baby" so I could not finish this.

Just after we got home, a Mr. Thompson brought us a box containing two dozen of apples. They were sent [by] two gentlemen who have visited here a number of times. I can tell you the apples were a great treat to us.

Lucia and I have done our washing today. We do not get at [it] very early in the morning so we do not get through very early.

Did I write you that we have a nice "sugar cured" ham given us a week or two ago? The people here are very kind to us. Henry wants me to tell you about my sleigh ride. He harnessed one of his mules and hitched it to a cutter. We had bells too, and took Sidney, Pauline, and myself about two miles up Grasshopper Creek. We all enjoyed it very much for it is not often that we have had a chance to ride. Today Henry is hauling logs for a man to build an ice house with. He now thinks that he and Charlie Sackett will get the "job" of filling the ice house. If they do it will be a good thing for them.

The children have all had a number of sleigh rides. Ask Martha if she knows that she will [be] thirty-eight years old next Saturday? Just think, almost forty years old. Don't it make you feel old to think of it? How are they all at Clement's and Benja's? I would like to spend the evening with you all but it is much too far to go there tonight.

Remember me to all the friends, Mother. I wish you could write to me. I should think a great deal of a letter from you.

Mary

Bannack City
Jan. 29, 1865

Dear Sister,

I expected to have written to [you] by the last mail but I could not write Sunday so put it off until Monday. The baby was taken sick Sunday night with a cold and has almost had lung fever. She was quite sick until Friday when she commenced getting better.

I was getting supper last Friday and went out to get some wood. I slipped down and strained my left wrist very badly. I have not been able to use my hand or hardly move my arm since until today. I can use my <u>fingers</u> a little. I am glad that the baby is so much better, for I don't know how I could have taken care of her if she was so sick now as she was last week. Tell Lucy that I "doctored" her with that homeopathic medicine that she gave me. If I had been in Tallmadge I should hardly have dared to have "perscribed" for her, but did not like to send for a new doctor. (The one we have always employed was not at home), so thought I would go by the "book" and she has got along very well.

The children have all had, or got, worse colds than they ever had in this country. I presume that I shall take my turn with the rest, but I have not had a cold since I left T. We had <u>very cold</u> weather here last week but today it is very pleasant and thaws quite fast.

The mail came in today but brought no letters for us. We have not had any letter from <u>any</u> of you for more than a month. I know that you must have written, but I do not understand why we do not get your letters. Charlie and Richard get letters almost every mail.

Tuesday. The children are all better; my arm or wrist is getting better so that I can dress myself without help. I have but a few minutes to write and the mail closes tonight. So I must say goodby.

Charlie and Richard now expect to go on to a farm near Virginia soon to get ready to raise vegetables next summer. Henry received a letter from his mother today, He is well. Don't forget to send the turnips and tomato seed that I wrote for. Love to all,

Mary

Bannack
Feb. 19, 1865

Dear Mother,

I received a letter from Martha last Friday, written December 30. I did not expect to get any letter for some time, for the Indians are so troublesome on the plains that I supposed that the mail would have to go by California, and it would take some time for it to reach here. I was very glad to hear again from home.

Since the Legislature adjourned it has been very quiet here. We have an evening now and then to ourselves. Mr. Edgerton has commenced reading "Healeys History of the War," aloud evenings, but we have so many interruptions we do not get along very fast with it. The children are all very much interested in hearing it read. They (the children) commenced their lessons again last week. I am afraid that when we go back to the States they will be behind all their schoolmates for they do not feel as much interested in their books when they study at home as they would if they were in school. I suppose that Alla and Howard and Charlie go to school all the time. They must be pretty good scholars by this time.

How is your lameness now? Do you get any better? I hope that when the warm weather comes you will be well again.

It seems as if spring would never come here. Last year at this time there was no snow here except on some of the higher mountains, and the weather was very mild, and now the snow is at least six inches deep and the weather is cold. I hope it will not last much longer. Those who are travelling to the States must have a hard time, but the coach is full every week of men who are going back and all the seats are engaged for a number of weeks.

I think that I shall have a chance to send the baby's picture to you before long. She has changed a great deal since it was taken — has grown prettier. She can sit alone now, has two upper and two under teeth, We are all well except Lucia. She has a cold, as all the rest of us have had. The Sunday school commenced today. Our children all attend. Lucia is one of the teachers. There were about twenty scholars today; many more will attend when it is warm weather. We heard from Hattie last week, all well.

Sunday night. I have got the supper and undressed the baby and now will try to finish this letter. If I could talk with you I could tell you about a great many things that would interest you, but it is another thing to write so that you would be interested. Martha (in her letter) asked if it would be safe to send a dress to the baby by mail. It might be perfectly safe, but I do not think she had better send it. It will be some time before I shall put short dresses on her and I have enough of them such as they are, to last some time. She (Baby) would soon learn to creep but I do not like to put her on the floor much as it is so cold.

We have not heard from Charlie or Richard since they left here. Henry was riding one of his mules and it threw him off and hurt his right shoulder (bruised it). Think he will get over it in a few days. My wrist is much better but is not well. It is swollen yet and pains me a good deal in the night. I presume it would not if I did not try to use it. I think often of your wrist that used to trouble you so much. Does it trouble you yet? Give love to all.

Mary

Bannack
March 6, 1865

Dear Mrs. Carter,

[Lucia Darling begins the letter] Aunt Mary does not know that she will have time to write you this eve., as the baby is so worrysome. If the baby is more quiet soon, I will give this into her hands to finish. She (the Baby) has been sick and is just well enough to be cross.

[Mrs. Edgerton continues from this point.] I tell Lucia that it will spoil the looks of my letters to have her commence it for she writes so much better than I do. Mattie is holding Baby while I write and I will have to hurry while she (Baby) is quiet. She has worried [me] more during the last ten days than all put together since she was born. She took cold, sitting on the floor, and was <u>very sick four</u> days and is not well now but is so much better that we think she is about well. Her teeth trouble her now.

We did not wash today but attended the funeral of a lady, the wife of one of our nearest neighbors. She was taken with convulsions about ten hours after giving birth to a child and had them as often as once every half hour for twenty-four hours when <u>she died</u>. <u>The child is doing well</u>.

Tell Mother that the gentleman who was going to take that picture to her has not gone to the states but will go before long.

The Snow is so deep between here and Salt Lake that our mail is much behind the time. I do hope that we shall have warmer weather before long. We have had such a long, long, cold winter. I am tired of it. I cannot write half that I would like to tonight for want of time.

I sent you a paper with the governor's veto to [a] bill that our Copperhead Legislature passed in which it was provided that where <u>white</u> men were the litigants, no man who had one-eight of African blood would be permitted to testify, but where black men were the litigants both black and white could testify. You will perceive that it (the veto) <u>is slightly</u> "sarcastical," but a majority of the <u>Members</u> don't know it to this day.[1]

I have written so fast that I presume I have made many mistakes. I have written very poorly. We are all very anxious to get news from the states, hope the mail will get in tonight and bring lots of letters.

I heard from Hattie last week. Willie had been quite sick with a cold but was better; the rest "all well." Mattie is about tired of holding Baby so I will have to take her (Baby). . . . Write often. I presume if I could see this by daylight I would not send it. Love to all, particularly to Mother. How I would like to see you all. Goodnight.

Mary

Bannack
March 19, 1865

Dear Sister,

I do not know whether you will ever get this letter if I write it but will write as if I thought you would receive it. It has been a <u>long</u> time since we have had any mail from the States, and I do not know that there is any prospect of the stages running again on the plains this spring.

I sent a short letter to Mother with the baby's picture by Mr. Thompson, who started for the States last Thursday. He will take a boat which is advertized to start on the first of April at Fort Benton and go down the river. I hope he will call on you on his way to New York.

---

[1] Edgerton vetoed the bill because of its discrimination against minorities, but both houses easily overrode the veto and the bill became law in spite of Edgerton's objections.

I wonder if spring has come to you yet? It does seem as if we should never have warm weather again. We shall all rejoice when it grows warmer. We have had a long cold winter; I think that streams and rivers will be very high when the snow melts, we have had so much of it. The baby has waked so I will have to stop writing for tonight.

Monday afternoon, 1 o'clock. We have finished our washing and now will try to finish this letter, but my hands feel so stiff and clumsy that it is not very pleasant business.

The day has been very pleasant and quite warm compared to the weather we have had. People are leaving here almost daily for new diggings where they think they will make money faster than here, but many will be disappointed I presume.

It is possible that we may move into some of the valleys this summer but I do not know whether we shall or not. Mr. Edgerton is going into Jefferson and Edgerton counties as soon as it is warmer weather to look at the country and see where he would like to live. It is very much warmer in the valleys than here, and I think we should like to live there better, particularly in the winter. I do not think we can find a healthier place than this is. We have but very little sickness here.

I suppose by this time you are looking around in your yard to see what is coming up. I would like to be with you. Are those roses alive that are in Nellie's yard? I never had any flowers that I thought more of than I did of those. They were such little tender roots when I got them and I had to watch them so closely to make them live. Have you kept any house plants through the winter? How does that Oleander that I left prosper?

The daguerreon was in here this morning and said he would like a picture of our house the first pleasant day. When he does I will send one to you. I wish we could have the inside of the house taken too so you could see just how we look and live here. I must close and if I have time will write a few lines to Howard and Alla for Pauline. . . .

Mary

Bannack
March 20, 1865[2]

Dear Howard and Alla, Charlie and Frannie and Mary Freeman,

How do you all do? I wish you were here to play with me this afternoon, it is so pleasant. We could go into the office and run and make as much noise as we have a mind to.

Wright and Sidney have commenced a snow fort. (I helped to roll some of the balls to make it with.) But I am afraid that it will melt before they can finish it.

We have got three hens and one rooster. We have put some shavings (we have not got any straw or hay) in a box for a nest so when they get ready to lay eggs they can go in the box. We had some more chickens but it was so cold that two froze to death and one froze its legs so that it (the leg) came off up by its feathers, so we had it killed. We didn't eat it though but the Indians did. They pick off all the dead chickens and pigs and all the old bones and bits of meat that the hogs don't get and carry them up to their Wickeyups, and cook and eat them. Do you think you would like to eat such dirty stuff? I know I shouldn't. I don't like to have them come into the house, they are so dirty.

Do you go to school now? I wish I could go with you for I don't like to recite alone as well as I should if I was in a class with others.

I do not remember much about Mary Freeman, but I know that I should like to play with her and with all the rest of you. We children all go to Sunday School and Lucia is one of the teachers. Mamma has to stay home to take care of the baby.

Wright is making a little boat and when the creek thaws we expect to [have] great fun sailing it, but I think I would rather play with you than sail a boat or do anything else. I think and talk a great deal about you, and often wish that I was in Tallmadge. Good night. Write soon to

Pauline

[2] This letter is written by Mrs. Edgerton on behalf of her young daughter Pauline, to some of Pauline's former playmates.

Monday afternoon

March 27, 1865

Martha,

I have just got through washing and as the baby is asleep I will write a few lines to you. You wrote about those things in the trunk. When we got the last black trunk the lock was broken and the straps were nearly broken, and I think it probable that some things had been taken out. I thought I would like to <u>know</u> about it. [I] do not care for the things, but thought it possible they were not put in the trunk. I am very sure that I wrote you that Pauline's balmoral came in the first trunk. She thinks a great deal of it. It was just what she needed. The arnica was in the first trunk but no glycerin. You asked if the <u>lemons</u> did any damage. No, but they were pretty well dried up and so were the flowers. If Mr. Edgerton had brought that trunk right through with him, I think they would have been perfectly fresh.

So you think this climate don't agree with me? I guess you would not say so if you should see me now. I have not been weighed lately but I think I am as fleshy as I ever was.

Sidney wants me to write to Howard that we have got a little calf and his mother is the prettiest white cow he ever saw (it is one we drove across the plains). Another thing is that one of our hens laid its first egg yesterday. The children are all <u>very much</u> pleased to think that <u>their</u> chickens will lay eggs.

Mr. Edgerton says that he will send that message whenever it is printed. The only copy we have had I sent to some of you. Think it was to Clem. How is he now?

I am so tired that I think I will not write any more today. I intend to write to some of you every week but sometimes do not have time to do so. Tell Mrs. **Seward** that Henry did receive all that was sent to him. I supposed that he had written about it or I should have done so.

Love to all

Mary

Bannack

April 2, 1865

Dear Mother,

The "mails" have commenced running again and we received letters from Martha, Homer and Mary, last week, and Lucia got one from Bell and Wright one from Sammy. We were glad to get them all. It seems good to hear from home once more. We expect to have mail three times a week after this, but I am afraid they will not be very regular for some time for the snow is very deep on the mountains between this place and Salt Lake.

We are all well. The baby grows "cute" and pretty every day. Pauline and the boys are "fat" and healthy. To tell the truth we are none of us very poor (in flesh I mean). I would much rather sit and talk with you tonight than write for I do not feel much in the writing mood.

Monday. I have a little time to write before it is time to get supper. It is a cold and cloudy day but we have done our washing. We have had very pleasant weather during the past week and the snow is almost gone in the valleys, but the streams are still covered with ice. The ice is so thick on the mill dam that loaded wagons cross over it every day.

Sidney has just come from the post office and says that they are going to send the mail out tonight so I will have to hurry to finish this. I have nothing in particular to write about but think you will want to hear from us whether we write any news or not. At present everything is at a "standstill" in the business line here. Miners are waiting for the streams to thaw so that they can wash the dirt they have been digging through the winter, and the merchants owing to the scarcity of things, have raised the prices on almost everything. Flour is now $38.00 (gold) a sack [100 pounds], sugar, $1.00 per pound, and other things in proportion. But this cannot last long, for there are a number of large trains loaded with flour and groceries that started from Salt Lake last fall for this place and Virginia, and got as far as Snake River where they were "snowed in" and have had to stay there through the winter. A great many of their cattle died (starved or froze to death) but men are going from here with teams to bring their loads here and will be here before long.

I presume that Henry has got to Ft. Benton by this time. I don't know whether he will wait there until the boats come up the river so that he can have a load back or not. If he does, [he] will not be back for some time. We have heard that many are already on the way to this territory. Some who were here last year expected to start on the first of the month.

Well I must stop writing and send this to the office or it will be too late for today's mail. Remember us to Mr. and Mrs. Seward and other friends. Pauline sends love to you and Alla particularly.

Mary

Bannack
April 9, 1865

Dear Sister,

I received your letter dated February 17th on last Friday. I think that you have all been having just such a time with colds as we have had. I hope to hear that Mother is much better. . . .

You wonder about the "cold weather that the thermometer was ten degrees below zero." That is nothing here. Why last week the thermometer "said ten degrees below zero" at least three mornings, but we do not feel the cold any more than you do in the spring when the ground freezes a little at night, and I do not believe that we feel as <u>chilly</u>. But when the "thermo." stands day after day at <u>forty</u> degrees below zero as it has here this last winter, <u>then we feel it</u>.

There was a man in here last night from the "Gallatin" valley who said that many of the farmers there had sowed their spring wheat more than two weeks ago.³ It is much warmer in the valleys than it is here.

Did you ever get my letter where I told you about the potatoes that we had? We have heard from Charlie and Richard but three times since they left here. Henry expected to visit them on his way

---

³ The center of the Gallatin Valley was a hundred miles northeast of Bannack. Farmers quickly settled the area and began producing crops for sale in the mining camps.

to Fort Benton. I don't know but they will feel somewhat discouraged because our spring is so "backward" here, but from all I can learn, winter "holds on" longer than usual everywhere.

I am not at all surprised to hear of Mr. Hinman's marriage, but think that "Marcia" was too good for him. You asked if I had worn out my morning dress? No, I have worn it all winter in the mornings and it has done me a great deal of good. I have almost worn out that [word indecipherable] dress that Louise made for me last Spring, and [I have] worn the darkest calico some. The other one I have saved for next summer but will have to put it on before long. Mattie has just finished a dark calico dress for herself. She sewed every stitch of it and made it very well. I wonder if Mary has grown as she (Mattie) has. Lucia is only half an inch taller than Mattie. The children have all grown three inches taller than they were when Mr. Edgerton went to the States.

I made those "ingrediencies" into ink last week. This last page and part of the one before is written with some of it. I like it very much. We expect another mail tonight, I hope we shall hear from home again. . . .

We are all well. The baby grows cunning every day. I wish you could see her. She is so full of fun. We all think there never was another such a baby and I guess she thinks so too, for she likes to be noticed and played with. I expect that we shall spoil her by paying her so much attention.

Mattie says "are you almost through writing?" so I will have to stop writing for tonight. Write often to Mary. Love from all to all.

> Mary

> Monday morn.
> April 10.

I have been washing. Have got all the white clothes washed and part of them boiled. Lucia is rinsing them while I have been getting the baby asleep. Mattie has washed the dishes and is now cleaning up her room. She and Pauline sleep in the middle room. We have to go through it to go into the kitchen.

Did I write you that we had some dagarreotype views of the scenery back of our house, also a picture of our house? They were taken since Mr. Thompson left here or I would have sent them to you.

The mail came in this morning but [I] did not get any letter from home. I was disappointed, for I am very anxious to hear how Mother is. Hope I shall hear soon. Spring is a hard time for old people. I was in hope that Mother would escape sickness this spring. Today is the mildest day we have had and I hope we shall have more such days now for I am tired of cold weather.

Heard from Wilbur's folks last week, were all well. Have not heard from Junius lately but suppose that he is at Helena, Edgerton Co.[4] He went with the "portable saw mill" that Wilbur owns a part of. Wilbur is making money fast.

Have I written you that the Legislature raised Mr. Edgertons' salary twenty-five hundred dollars, making his whole salary five thousand dollars (greenbacks)? He has not received one dollar of pay from [the] Government since his appointment as Governor. The only communications he can get from W. [Washington] are in reference to a "special Indian agent" who was sent here. He started sometime last July with a number of wagons loaded with goods for the "natives" but has not arrived here yet. We have heard of him a number of times, but not from him.

Have you all turned to "oil" in the States? Most of the letters received here lately have wonderful accounts of the oil wells.

Wednesday. Wright has concluded to send his letter to Sammy by itself so I will not wait to write any more but [will] send it today. I received that message of Caleb Lyons of "Lyonsdale" (as he always signs all of his papers and letters). We had had it before and I thought of sending it to you, but thought perhaps you had never heard of him so I did not send it. They have great times with him in Idaho.[5] Write soon. Love to all.

Mary

4 Gold was discovered in Last Chance Gulch, 125 miles northeast of Bannack, in July, 1864. In the fall, a miners' meeting named the new settlement Helena.

5 Caleb Lyon of New York, became Idaho's territorial governor on February 24, 1864.

Bannack

April 16, 1865

Dear Mother,

I have not written to you for some time, and the last time I wrote in a great hurry. I have nothing in particular to write but will write so that you may not forget that you have a daughter living here in the Rocky Mountains. I think when you are around visiting your children, you had better make me a good long visit. I am sure that I should be as glad to see you and visit with you as any of them (the children) could be.

I would like to know just how you all are today? The mail is behind time today, when it comes I shall expect to hear from some of you. I hope to hear that you are well. In Martha's last letter she wrote that you were sick with a cold.

April 23rd. I had written so far when I had to stop and get supper, and I thought I should have time to finish it in the evening but could not get the time. I have been very busy during the past week, making pants for the boys; finished them last night . I should have taken time to have finished this but I have been waiting thinking that I should get a letter from some of you at home. But [I] have not received any letter for nearly three weeks. I hope none of you are sick.

Sidney just came in and said "the mail is coming in" so I will wait to see if we get a letter.

I have got a letter from Martha dated March 19th and Mattie received letters from Homer and Mary. We were very glad to get them to hear that you were better and the rest of them were well.

We also heard that President Lincoln and Secretary Seward had been assassinated. It is terrible to think of it! What do these traitors expect to gain by such deeds? I never saw Mr. Edgerton so excited about anything as he is about this. I do not wonder at it for it is enough [to] excite anyone. What a shock there must have been all through the States.

It is when we hear such news that we wished we lived where we could get "earlier" news. We are all well. Martha asks if Henry Tilden is going home this spring? We did not know that he thought of it when he left here (he hired a spring wagon to go with) for he said that he should be back in four or six weeks (when the boats got to Ft. Benton). I shall think it very strange if he does go, and shall not believe it until [I] hear that he has gone. There is a boat expected at Fort Benton on the first or tenth of May. I did think that I would not send another letter to you that is written in a hurry. I shall have to close this and send it to the office or it will be too late. Will try to answer Martha's letter sometime this week. Love to all from

Mary

Bannack
May 7, 1865

Dear Mother,

I received your letter last week. I do not want you to think that I let Mattie attend all the "Balls" we have here, for it is not so. I should be the last one to be willing to have her associate with the "set" that generally attend them. Those she attended (she has been twice) were <u>select</u> <u>parties</u>; none of the drinking, loafing set were allowed to go. There have been a number of such parties and there had been a good deal said because Lucia and Mattie did not go; thought the reason was because they belonged to the governor's family and they felt above those who attended them, as they had refused all invitations.

At this time I was urged very hard to let Mattie go. Lucia went with her, so I consented with the understanding that she should not attend another during the winter, and it was the last. Everything passed off very pleasantly and for that reason they stayed much later than they intended.

You spoke of Mattie's age? I know that she is only fourteen years old, but it is very hard to convince people here that she is under eighteen. She is so large. I think that if you had been here, Mother, you would have done as I did taking all things into consideration. There are no parties here except dancing parties, and there is no other amusement of any kind.

Sunday, May 14, 1865. When I commenced this I thought I would finish it the next day, but Mr. Edgerton came home from

Virginia and said that he should move to V. as soon as a house could be fixed for us which would probably be in two or three weeks, so we <u>women</u> have been very busy sewing during the past week. I am glad that we are going to live near Hattie and there are many other reasons why it will be pleasanter and better for us to live in V.

The people there expect to purchase or build a house for us and then Mr. Edgerton can have all the "Law" business that he can attend to with good fees. There is a greater variety of everything there and things are cheaper than here. I presume that it will not seem so much like <u>home</u> there for some time as it does here, but I am glad that we are going to move, not that I like the moving part but I think I shall like the <u>change</u>.[6]

Pauline has got over having [a] sore mouth. She was very sick for a week. The rest of us are well. Mr. Edgerton expects to go to Helena (about one hundred and fifty miles from here) in a few days. He will probably be gone over a week. Junius lives there and we have heard that Henry Tilden is there. [I] don't know what he is doing; he has been there for some weeks.

It snowed all last night and has been snowing fast all day. It is not cold but it seems like cold to see so much snow. Baby creeps around and pulls up the lounge and by chairs but can't stand alone yet. She has a <u>little bod</u>y but is plump and fat. I think she looks very much as Frankie did but is not as large. . . . Have not had any letter from home in nearly two weeks.

[I] will send a paper not because it is a late paper but because it has the "winding up" of the Legislature here. Thought you might like to read it. In Mary's last letter to Mattie were letters

[6] It is not clear who was behind the move to bring Edgerton to Virginia City, nor is it clear why the Edgertons did not move there. On November 26, 1864, the *Montana Post* noted that a subscription list was being circulated for "the purpose of purchasing a fine private residence to be presented to our Governor, as a token of regard from the Citizens of Virginia. We hope soon to hear of the requisite amount being raised, and have no doubt of the Governor's changing his residence from Bannack to our city." Probably this effort was related to Virginia City's successful campaign in the first legislature to replace Bannack as the territorial capital. On May 6, 1865, the *Post* noted that Edgerton had arrived in town, and expressed the hope "that our citizens will make an effort to induce him to stay among us. We cannot help thinking that this is his proper place, and we feel sure that a large majority of the people are of the same opinion."

from Howard to Wright and Sidney. They were very glad to get them and will write to him when we get to V. . . . Love to all from all.

Mary

Bannack
May 21, 1865

Dear Sister,

I received your letter dated April 7th last night, and one dated April 11th nearly a week ago. I was very <u>agreeably</u> surprised to hear that you had sent a box of <u>good</u> things to us. I had not expected anything of the kind, but I can tell you we shall be very glad to get them. And the lard <u>will be very acceptable.</u>

Three weeks ago I bought eleven pounds of lard, paid eighty cents per lb. for it. Everything is much higher here in the spring than at any other time. You may be surprised to hear that we have paid seventy-five dollars for a sack (one hundred pounds) of flour, but two days after we could have bought it for $60 and now it is only forty-five dollars a sack. Cheap isn't it?

The snow has been so deep and the roads so bad between Salt Lake and this place that those who have had flour on the road could not get over the "divide" with wagons, but had to pack everything over. At one time there was not a pound of flour to be bought in this town and many families lived on meat and dried fruit (if they had any). The first flour that was brought in sold for one dollar a pound. I did not write you about it at the time for fear you would think we were on the point of starvation. But we have had plenty of the necessaries of life and we can get along very well without the luxuries. I don't know how we shall ever pay you for what you have sent us.[7]

[7] The flour shortage was felt throughout Montana in the winter of 1864–65, and as the supply dwindled, prices rose. Flour which normally sold for approximately $25.00 for a 100-pound sack had climbed to $100.00 by mid-April, as speculators bought up local supplies and forced prices up. On April 2, a mob in Nevada City confiscated flour, paid the merchants for it at the old rates, and then sold it, again at the old rates, to citizens. On that day and the following day, mass meetings were held on the subject in Virginia City, but the sheriff broke them up. But on Tuesday, April 19, a carefully organized

Mr. Edgerton has gone to Helena, shall look for him back the last of this week or the first of next week. We heard from Junius last week. He is in Helena and likes living there. Says he shall stay a <u>year</u> at least. Said that Henry was there working for them. I don't know how long he expects to stay there. Shall know when Mr. Edgerton gets back.

Since Mr. E. went away, we have heard great stories about the Indians killing the whites who were on their way to Ft. Benton. I don't know how much truth there is in the reports, but if they are true, Mr. E. will raise a company of men while in Helena to go after the Indians.[8] I hope he will not have to go, but <u>I do want to have</u> the Indians killed. I think that if the government would station men (soldiers) at different points on the river and on the plains instead of fitting out an expedition like Crawford and Sully to cross the plains every year and of no earthly use, it would benefit the Territories much more and cost [the] government less.

We are all well. Heard from Charlie and Richard a few days ago and they were well. I sent them and Mr. Cowan who crossed the plains with us some of those seeds you sent me. Mr. Edgerton

group of five hundred men made a systematic search of Virginia City and confiscated all the flour they could find. They then rationed it to the citizens, on the basis of need, selling it at the standard price. They then gave the money to the merchants from whom they had taken the flour. Shortly thereafter, flour began arriving again from Utah and the price quickly dropped to normal levels. See the *Montana Post*, April 8, 15, and 22, 1865. See also, Dorothy M. Johnson, "Flour Famine in Alder Gulch, 1864," *Montana, The Magazine of Western History*, VII (Winter, 1957), 18–27; and Dorothy Winner, "Rationing During the Montana Gold Rush," *Pacific Northwest Quarterly*, XXXVI (April, 1945), 115–20.

[8] The Indian difficulty resulted after some trouble in Fort Benton during which some whites killed three Indians. On May 25, the Indians retaliated, killing ten white wood cutters near there. Rumors flew through the territory that the Indians were on the rampage. On June 10, the *Montana Post* printed a letter from the scene, warning that "there is but little safety here." The paper demanded the "obliteration of these barbarians." Mass meetings were held in Virginia City and Helena to discuss the situation, and Edgerton wired the War Department for troops (see *The War of the Rebellion: A Compilation of the Official Records of the Union and Confederate Armies* [Washington, D.C., 1897], Series I, Vol. 48, p. 690). On May 31, he issued a proclamation calling out a volunteer militia of five hundred men. Few men volunteered despite pleas at several meetings by both Edgerton and Sanders, and in the end, on June 6, Edgerton called off the operation. He returned home to Bannack, and the summer of 1865 passed peacefully in Montana.

took one package of seeds with him to give to a number who have spoken for some of the turnip seed.

We have had one-half day of rain and the "Grasshopper" has "overflew" its banks and washed away the footbridge that crossed the creek near us to Yankee Flats, and the poor <u>Yankee Flaters</u> have to go quite a distance above and cross over on the wagon bridge or bridges of the wagon road (whichever you please) to come into town. The stream is very high and sounds quite like a river as it passes our house. I must stop now and get supper. If I have time before the mail goes out [I] will write to Lucy Ann. Mr. E. says that he will show you before long whether he can write or not. So look out.

My wringer has been mended so that I can use it very well. It is not as good as a new one, but it does very well. You don't know how sweet my letter was from that violet. I wish I could see your yard! The flowers are beginning to bloom here. Pauline found some of that sweet-scented grass. I will send you some of it. Your dress is a beautiful color. It must be very becoming to you. I wish mine was the same color but do not think that I can get it colored here very soon. Love to all,

Mary Edgerton

Bannack
June 4, 1865

Dear Sister Martha,

I received yours of April 24 nearly a week ago but have not had time to answer it. Lucia was taken sick with mountain fever a week ago last Friday and had a very high fever for two days, since has had no fever but is very weak. She is able to sit up some now but I presume it will be some time before she will be strong enough to do much.

[I] have had a slight "tech" of jaundice this spring. I have not been sick "mind you" only I grew yellow! The whites of my eyes were orange colors and my skin was nearly as yellow. Finally I took a dose of "Podophillynn," (Do you know what this is? If you don't, take a dose and you will never forget it) which helped me some, but I am not as <u>white</u> as I might be now and I do not feel very strong. I am able to <u>work</u> and Mattie and I have to work pretty hard "about these days."

Mr. Edgerton got back from Helena or Last Chance a week [ago] last night pretty well tired out. (Henry came with him.) He went to Virginia to try a lawsuit on Monday morning and expected to have come back last Thursday, but hearing that the Indians were attacking trains who were on their way to Fort Benton, he has issued a proclamation to raise men to go after the Indians. I don't know whether he is going with them or not, but suppose that he will. I have not heard <u>directly</u> from him since he left here. I looked for him some last night. I heard that the company were to start today but don't know whether it is so or not.

Junius received a letter from his sister while Mr. E. was in Helena, with the intelligence of the death of his brother Philo. He was a prisoner in Libby Prision. They suppose that he starved to death. <u>Junius</u> felt it terribly and so did Wilbur. He (W.) was here a week ago tonight on his way home from Salt Lake and Mr. Edgerton told him about it.

I wonder if it is cold in Ohio today? The tops of the mountains near us were white with snow this morning and the air is cold enough for snow tonight. We can see snow in the mountains in the distance all year round. I cannot finish this tonight, will write some tomorrow if I have time after washing. The mail will not go out again before Tuesday. In the meantime I may hear from Mr. Edgerton. I have to write to Abbie and to William but don't know when I shall get time to do so. We had a <u>good long</u> letter from William two weeks ago, and one from Abbie the week or two before. Shall answer them as soon as I can.

Tuesday eve. I have just finished making a sponge for I must bake and iron tomorrow. Today I have been trying to fix over my pink calico for Mattie [as] a dress. I guess I am going to have that slate colored berege made over for her for she has outgrown <u>everything</u> that she had last summer and I do not want to buy for her. I have so little time to sew that I don't know when I shall finish them. Perhaps will have them ready for next summer. Mr. Edgerton has <u>commenced</u> a letter to you. Don't know whether he will finish it so it can go in the next mail. I will send you the last *Montana Post*.

Tell Howard that Sidney was out riding horseback with "Mr. Butcher" the man that tends the "Overland" here and found seven prairie hen's eggs in a nest and Mr. E. brought them home in his handkerchief and we put them under a hen that was sitting and we expect to have some prairie chickens before long. Mr. E. thought the eggs must be spoiled by this time so he broke one today and found a little chicken in it. The eggs are not much larger than that Killder's egg and look very much like it. Sidney is nine years old today and Mr. E. bought a pony for the boys yesterday, paid eighty dollars for it. Surely that is a nice birthday present.

Write as often as you can. Love to all.

Mary

Bannack

July 10, 1865

Dear Sister Martha,

I received your letter dated June 5th (I think) last Saturday. I am glad to hear that you now have some fruit. Wish I could be with you and help eat it when ripe. . . . You ask if my sewing machine troubled me any? It has some when I tried to sew cotton cloth, but does not when I sew on wollen. I shall try to clean it for it needs it badly. I don't know whether I can get oil of turpentine here or not.

Mattie received that bead collar a long time ago and has written a number of times since, but I presume she forgot to say anything about it.

What did you do on the Fourth? We expected to have gone to "Bald Mountain," had our "fixings" all packed; the horse saddled for the girls to ride and the wagon ready for the rest of us, when it commenced raining. The children felt "terribly" about it, so after it stopped raining we concluded that we would go to the "Point of Rocks" ten miles from here where we went fishing a few weeks ago.

It rained a little after we started but we did not get wet much thanks to that silk "umbrella" we brought with us.

The girls rode pretty fast and Lucia felt very tired when we got there. She did not think that she was so strong as she was before she was sick. She rode back in the wagon. It grew quite cool while we were there and she (L.) took cold and was so lame that she could hardly stir for three or four days. She has not got entirely over it yet. Mattie rode back horseback and felt it some the next day, but nothing compared to Lucia.

Mr. Smith, our minister, took a load of his Sabbath school children to the same place that we were; two of the boys and Wright rode horseback with Lucia and Mattie. They had a very pleasant time. The children in particular enjoyed their picnic very much. I was afraid that the baby would be sick, that she would take cold; but she did not seem to feel it at all. She stands alone and has walked a number of steps today.

We have done a large washing today and I made biscuit and had a veal "pot pie" for supper. I shall have to stop writing now for it is getting too dark to write.

Wednesday. I did not write yesterday for the mail did not go out; will go tonight. I baked bread and cake yesterday and commenced a pair of pants for Wright and have finished them today. I made some for Sidney last week and have made them each a coat. It is more than I can do to make clothes as fast as they need them. You ask if we have heard from that box yet. No, but expect every day to hear that it is at Virginia. Lucia has just finished a letter for Lucy and Clem.

It has been very warm for a few days past but the nights are cool and pleasant. It does seem strange to have it so warm here and snow in sight all the time. If you think this is not written well, lay it to the baby, for she is pulling up by me all the time and it is as much as I can do to write at all. I would like very much to see your roses but I can't so [I] will imagine how they look. I must send this to the office now. Love to all.

Mary

Bannack

Aug. 7, 1865

Dear Mother,

I will try to write to you today but really do not know what to write to make my letter interesting to you or to anyone. Lucia and Mattie have gone on a "berrying" excursion so we put off our washing until tomorrow. They expect to get gooseberries and perhaps rasberries. The gooseberries are different from any that I ever saw. They are large, oblong, and when ripe are a dark color almost like the color of whorttleberries and very sour like ripe currents. I like them very much but they require a great deal of sugar to sweeten them. I think if they were cultivated they would grow much larger. I have saved seed and will try them. Mr. Edgerton went to Virginia last Saturday, shall expect him back Friday night.

The "Hon. Mr. Ashley" just arrived here (in town, I mean) from Virginia City.[9] He is on his way back to the States — leaves tonight I believe. Wright's "partner" has gone to Virginia City, so he is "first postmaster" and Henry is his assistant. Sidney goes to the office occasionally to see how they are getting along.

Pauline is playing with the baby while I am writing. She (the baby) walks now most of the time — when she is in a "hurry" she creeps. How does your baby boy get along?[10] Is he quiet? I suppose that he has grown and improved in looks since Homer wrote to Mattie. (Tell him (Homer) that [we] received his letter last Saturday.)

I received two letters from Martha a week ago. In one of them there was a collar for me for which I am thankful. I think it is very pretty. I am afraid that I cannot finish this to go in the mail tonight. I must stop now and get supper. I churned this morning three and a half pounds of butter. [I have] churned three times in two weeks. I make all the butter that we use now and it is first rate butter too. Would like to have you try some of it. We have but one cow now.

[9] James M. Ashley was a congressman from Ohio and was chairman of the House Committee on Territories at the time the Montana Territory was created. He named the territory and was instrumental in its creation.

[10] The reference is to Martha Carter's infant son, Mrs. Wright's grandson.

Wednesday. I did not get any time to write yesterday. The baby was quite sick the night before last with diarrhea. I did not have much chance to sleep, she was so restless. I gave her some charcoal and brandy and she is much better today but not entirely well. We washed yesterday and baked today.

Whenever Mr. Edgerton goes away, something happens so that we want him very much. Last night our cow was sick and we thought she would die. She was so bloated that she could hardly breathe. Henry got some men to help him give her melted lard and it helped her so she seems well this morning. We suppose that she had eaten alkali. I expect Mr. Edgerton home tomorrow.

We heard that our box is on the [way] here from the river. Hope we shall get it this week. Had a letter from Hattie yesterday. All well. We had some large, new potatoes given us for supper Sunday night. They grow in the garden opposite us that I have written to you about. I suppose you are having plenty of every vegetable now. We shall have soon, but we do not raise them ourselves. If we had not expected to have moved to Virginia in the spring, we should have had a garden of our own. We might have had one just as well as not. We are so near the creek that it would not have been much work to irrigate it.

Tell Martha that she must not give up writing to me if she has got a new baby to take care of. I want her to write once a week if she can. Tell Lucy Ann and Mr. Shaw that we have not heard from them very lately. Love to all from all.

Mary

Bannack

August 20, 1865

Dear Sister,

I wrote last week to Lucy Ann and today will commence a letter to you and finish it when I can. We did not get any letters from you last week but hope to hear from you this week. We are all well. Have had pretty warm weather for a few days past. I can think of nothing now to write you that would be interesting.

131

There is just as much excitement here about gold and silver lodes as ever. New ones are being discovered every week and almost every day. I saw some rock from a silver lode the other day that had [been] heated so I could see pure silver like fine wire all through it. There is no machinery here yet for getting the silver from the rock but I believe there is some on the way here. The machinery is very different from that used in getting gold from rock. There are a number of scientific men who have visited other mining countries here from N.Y. Most of them represent some mining company there. They are here to examine the "lodes" and put up mills. They all talk <u>very favorably</u> of the mines in this country.

After supper. The girls are gone to sing with the Sabbath School and a few others who meet to sing an hour so that the scholars can learn the tunes. We had a letter from Charlie Sackett last week. He was in good spirits and says they are doing "first rate." They will make money on their ranch. We have green peas and new potatoes. Charlie writes that they have everything in the vegetable line from cucumbers to new potatoes and wants us to visit them.

Monday. I have just finished washing and am very tired, too tired to write much — but I want to send this in the mail tonight. Henry and Sidney have just got back from Sturgis's mill with a load of lumber. Sidney thinks it has been a long day.

The children received a present today of three apples and one peach. The baby is perfectly crazy after the apples. I suppose you have plenty of them now; would like to help eat them. How does that baby get along? Have you named him yet? Do you hear from Mr. and Mrs. Gardner nowadays? We have never answered that long letter from Mr. G. yet. I have so little time to write that it is about all I can do to write to you at home and then I do not write very often, not as often as I like to get letters. . . .

Give my best love to Mother. How I would like to see her and you all. Love to all. Have not had time to look this over.

Mary

Bannack
August 27, 1865

Dear Sister Martha,

I do not feel much like writing today, but because it is Sunday and I have a little time that I <u>can</u> write, [I] will commence a letter. I am not sick but <u>lazy</u>. We have had very warm weather for more than a week past and it makes us all unfit for work.

We did not get any letter from you last week. It has been more than two weeks since we have heard from any of you. Have you written or is your time so much occupied with that "boy" that you cannot write. If you cannot write get Homer or Mary to write for you. We want to hear from you at least once a week.

Lucia commenced teaching last week; has sixteen scholars. Don't know how long she will keep it up. Sidney and Pauline attend school. Wright has to be in the (Post) office so much that he cannot go to school.

Lucia received a letter from her sisters last week. One of them, "Tina," has been very sick but is much better now. They wrote that Volney Edgerton and all his family were going to visit in Marshall Mich. in September.[11] I wish we could visit there with them. If we could get aboard the cars <u>here</u> and go there we <u>might</u> do so.

I hope it shall not be many years before we can have a railroad through this territory to the Pacific Coast. Then you may expect a visit from us and we shall expect you here.

It is raining very hard now, has hailed some. Think it will be cooler after the shower. We do not have such heavy showers very often. We expect Wilbur here sometime this week. Don't know whether Hattie will come with him or not. He is coming over to make a speech at a political meeting. Our election comes off next week, Monday, Sept. 4. I don't know how the election will go but presume that the Copperheads will elect their ticket, for all Missouri is here.

The soldiers that are coming into the Territory this fall will not get here soon enough to vote. The law is every voter shall have been in the territory sixty days previous to election.

[11] Volney Edgerton was Sidney Edgerton's brother.

Major Upson, Indian agent, is the Union candidate for delegate to Congress. McLean, the same that was delegate last year, [is] the Democrat or Copperhead candidate.

After supper. The girls have been to the "Sing" this eve., but did not find any others there so they came back. There are only a few here now that take any interest in the Sunday school. We have no minister here now. Mr. Smith (the minister) who had been here, is now in Virginia City. I don't know whether there is one coming here this year or not. Those who are sent out by the Home Missionary Society cannot begin to live here on the salary allowed by the society — everything is so high.

It is almost time for the mail to close so I will have to send this to the office. I hope we shall hear from you this week. We are all well. The baby walks and is in all sorts of mischief. Write soon. Tell Lucy Ann to write too whenever she can. Do you hear from [?]? Love to all.

Mary

Epilogue

*I*N HER LATER YEARS, Mattie Edgerton recalled that she did not know "how the rest felt on leaving our mountain home, but I certainly experienced no regret." Neither, it may be certain, did her mother. Mrs. Edgerton's thoughts on leaving Montana have not survived, but her departure was swift, abrupt, and final; she must have been elated at the opportunity to return to Ohio. One may conjecture that she would have been extremely reluctant to leave Ohio and move to Montana a second time, and this reluctance may have also influenced Edgerton's decision not to return to the territory. When he resigned the Montana governorship, Edgerton closed the door on his political career. He went into private practice as a lawyer and continued to reside in Akron until his death in 1900.

Unfortunately, virtually nothing is known of Mrs. Edgerton's life after she left Montana. She became again an Akron housewife and no doubt was pleased at the prospect. After her return to Ohio, she did bear two more children, daughters whom she named Nina and Ione. In addition, she may have lost one more child in infancy. She returned to Montana only once, in 1882, to visit her eldest daughter who had married and returned to the territory. Two years later, on August 3, 1884, she died after a brief illness and was buried in Tallmadge.[1]

[1] *Akron Beacon Journal*, August 4, 1884.

Manuscript Sources

Unless otherwise noted, all of the following manuscript collections are in the archives of the Montana Historical Society in Helena.

Bannack Collection.

Conrad, Thomas. Papers, 1857–1899.

Darling, Lucia A. Lucia Darling Collection.

————. Diary of a Trip Across the Plains from Tallmadge, Ohio, to Bannack City, 1863.

Duncan, W. M. "First Public School in Montana." Typescript.

Dunn, William. "History and Production of the Bannack Mines." Typescript.

Edgerton Family Papers, 1859–1884.

Edgerton, Sidney, Papers, 1864–1892.

Fergus, James. Papers, 1834–1867. University of Montana Archives.

————. Papers, 1857–1926.

Harris, Alice R. Alice R. Harris Collection, 1866–1907.

Langford, Nathaniel P. "Address Delivered Before the Grand Lodge of Montana at the Third Annual Communication, in the City of Virginia, Oct. 8, 1867, by N. P. Langford, R. W. Historian."

————. Papers, 1863–1933.

Meredith, Emily. Letter from Bannack. 1863.

————. "Experiences and Impressions of a Woman in Montana, 1862–1863." Typescript.

Morley, James H. "Diary of James Morley in Montana, 1862–1865." Typescript.

Nuckolls, E. Letter to the *Tri-Weekly Miner's Register*, Central City, Colorado, December 28, 1862.

Oaths taken by the Members of the First Legislative Assembly of Montana.

Plassman, Martha Edgerton. "A Reminiscence of 1866." Typescript.

————. "Early Schools of Montana." Typescript.

————. "Excerpts from Letters of Mary Edgerton, 1863–1865." Typescript.

————. "How It Chanced." Typescript.

————. "How We Came Here." Typescript.

————. "Judge Edgerton's Daughter." Typescript.

————. "Pioneer Amusements." Typescript.

————. "Reminiscences." Typescript.

————. "Residence of Montana's First Governor." Typescript.

————. "Retrospect: Summer." Typescript.

————. "Retrospect: Winter." Typescript.

————. "Return Journey." Typescript.

Sanders, Harriet. "Diary of A Journey from Omaha to East Bannack City in the Summer of 1863 via Kearny, Laramie, South Pass, and Lower Snake Ferry." Typescript.

Sanders, Wilbur F. "The Beaverhead Country." Typescript.

————. "Early History of Montana." Incomplete manuscript.

————. "Notes on Montana History." Hubert H. Bancroft Collection, Bancroft Library.

————. "Sketches of Early Settlers in Montana." Typescript.

Toole, Jack. "The Founding of Bannack, Montana." Typescript.

Government Documents

Browne, J. Ross. *Report of J. Ross Brown on the Mineral Resources of the States and Territories West of the Rocky Mountains.* Washington: Government Printing Office, 1868.

————, and Taylor, James W. *Reports Upon the Mineral Resources of the United States.* Washington: Government Printing Office, 1867.

Fisk, Captain James L. *Expedition from Fort Abercrombie to Fort Benton.* 37th Congress, 3d Sess., 1862–63. House Executive Document No. 80.

Taylor, James W. *Report of James W. Taylor on the Mineral Resources of the United States East of the Rocky Mountains.* Washington: Government Printing office, 1868.

United States State Department. Territorial Papers, Montana Territory, 1864–1873.

United States War Department. *The War of the Rebellion: A Compilation of the Official Records of the Union and Confederate Armies.* Washington: Government Printing Office, 1897. Series I, Vol. 48.

Newspapers

Akron Beacon Journal (Akron, Ohio), 4 August 1884.

Montana Post (Virginia City), August 1864–September 1865.

Summit County Beacon (Akron, Ohio), 1858–1865.

Books

Bancroft, Hubert Howe. *History of Washington, Idaho and Montana, 1845–1889. The Works of Hubert Howe Bancroft*, Vol. 31. San Francisco: The History Company, Publishers, 1890.

Barsness, Larry. *Gold Camp: Alder Gulch and Virginia City, Montana.* New York: Hastings House, 1962.

Burlingame, Merrill G. *The Montana Frontier.* Helena: The State Publishing Company, 1942.

————, and Toole, K. Ross. *A History of Montana.* 3 Vols. New York: The Lewis Historical Publishing Company, 1957.

Campbell, J. L. *Idaho: Six Months in the Gold Diggings, The Emigrant's Guide Overland.* New York: Author, 1864.

Dickson, Arthur J., ed. *Covered Wagon Days: A Journey Across the Plains in the Sixties, and Pioneer Days in the Northwest, from the Private Journals of Albert Jerome Dickson.* Cleveland: Arthur J. Clark, 1929.

Dimsdale, Thomas J. *The Vigilantes of Montana or Popular Justice in the Rocky Mountains, Being a correct and impartial narrative of the Chase, Trial, Capture, and Execution of Henry Plummer's Road Agent Band, together with accounts of the Lives and Crimes of many of the Robbers and Desperadoes, the whole being interspersed with Sketches of Life in the Mining Camps of the "Far West."* 3d ed. Helena: The State Publishing Company, 1915.

Dimsdale, Thomas J. *The Vigilantes of Montana or Popular Justice in the Rocky Mountains, Being a Correct and Impartial Narrative of the Chase, Trial, Capture, and Execution of Henry Plummer's Road Agent Band together with accounts of the robbers and desperadoes, the whole being interspersed with sketches of life in the mining camps of the "Far West"; forming the only reliable work on the subject ever offered to the public.* Norman: University of Oklahoma Press, 1953.

Frazer, Robert W. *Forts of the West: Military Forts and Presidios, and Posts Commonly Called Forts, West of the Mississippi River to 1898.* Norman: University of Oklahoma Press, 1965.

Hamilton, James M. *From Wilderness to Statehood: A History of Montana, 1805–1900.* Edited by Merrill G. Burlingame. Portland: Binfords and Mort, 1957.

Howard, Joseph K. *Montana: High, Wide and Handsome.* New Haven: Yale University Press, 1959.

Jackson, W. Turrentine. *Wagon Roads West: A Study of Federal Road Surveys and Construction in the Trans-Mississippi West, 1846–1869.* New Haven: Yale University Press, 1965.

Johnson, Allen, ed. *Dictionary of American Biography,* Vol. 6. New York: Charles Scribner's Sons, 1956.

Langford, Nathaniel. *Vigilante Days and Ways: The Makers and Making of Montana, Idaho, Oregon, Washington, and Wyoming.* Edited by Dorothy M. Johnson. Missoula: University of Montana Press, 1957.

Leeson, Michael. *History of Montana, 1739–1885: A History of Its Discovery and Settlement, Social and Commercial Progress, Mines and Miners, Agriculture and Stock-Growing, Churches, Schools, and Societies, Indians and Indian Wars, Vigilantes, Courts of Justice, Newspaper Press,*

Navigation, Railroads and Statistics, with Histories of Counties, Cities, Villages and Mining Camps. Chicago: Warner, Beers and Company, 1885.

Miller, James K. P. *The Road to Virginia City: The Diary of James Knox Polk Miller.* Edited by Andrew Rolle. Norman: University of Oklahoma Press, 1960.

Miller, Joaquin. *An Illustrated History of Montana.* Chicago: The Lewis Publishing Company, 1894.

Raymer, Robert G. *Montana: The Land and the People.* 3 Vols. Chicago: The Lewis Publishing Company, 1930.

Sanders, Helen F. *A History of Montana.* 3 Vols. Chicago: The Lewis Publishing Company, 1813.

Stuart, Granville. *Forty Years on the Frontier as Seen in the Journals and Reminiscences of Granville Stuart, Gold-Miner, Trader, Merchant, Rancher and Politician.* Edited by Paul C. Phillips. 2 Vols. Cleveland: The Arthur H. Clark Company, 1925.

Toole, K. Ross. *Montana: An Uncommon Land.* Norman: University of Oklahoma Press, 1959.

Wheat, Carl I. *Mapping the Transmississippi West, 1540–1861.* 5 Vols. San Francisco: The Institute of Historical Cartography, 1960.

Articles

Archibald, Pauline W. "Mary Wright Edgerton." *Montana Magazine of History* 1 (1951):37–39.

Branch, E. Douglas. "Frederick West Lander, Road Builder." *Mississippi Valley Historical Review* 16 (1929):172–87.

Clark, W. A. "Centennial Address on the Origin, Growth, and Resources of Montana." *Contributions to the Historical Society of Montana* 2 (1896):45–60.

Derks, J. C. "The First Printing Press that Came to Montana." *Anaconda Standard*, 5 September 1899.

Edgar, Henry. "Journal of Henry Edgar — 1863." *Contributions to the Historical Society of Montana* 3 (1900):124–42.

Fergus, James. "A Leaf from the Diary of James Fergus Relative to the Fisk Emigration Party of 1862, and Early Mining Life at Bannack, 1863." *Contributions to the Historical Society of Montana* 2 (1896): 252–54.

————. "Early Mining Life at Bannack and Alder Gulch." *Rocky Mountain Magazine* 1 (1900):265–69.

Hedges, Cornelius. "Early Masonry in Montana." *Rocky Mountain Magazine* 1 (1900):13–17.

Johnson, Dorothy M. "Flour Famine in Alder Gulch." *Montana, The Magazine of Western History* 7 (1957):18–27.

Munson, Lyman E. "Pioneer Life in Montana." *Contributions to the Historical Society of Montana* 5 (1904):200–34.

Nichol, Ruth. "Lucia Aurora Darling, Pioneer Teacher." *Delta Kappa Gamma Bulletin*, June 1943.

Park, Mrs. S. W. [Lucia Darling]. "The First School in Montana." *Contributions to the Historical Society of Montana* 5 (1904): 187–95.

Peet, Herbert M. "Captain Rogers, Rebel Typical of Missourians Who Developed Montana." *Great Falls Tribune*, 7 August 1955.

Plassman, Martha. "Biographical Sketch of Hon. Sidney Edgerton, First Territorial Governor." *Contributions to the Historical Society of Montana* 3 (1900): 331–40.

————. "Martha Edgerton Plassman Writes Interesting Story." *Great Falls Tribune*, 23 October 1932.

Ronan, Peter. "Discovery of Alder Gulch." *Contributions to the Historical Society of Montana* 3 (1900): 143–52.

Sanders, Wilbur Edgerton. "Montana: Organization, Name and Naming." *Contributions to the Historical Society of Montana* 7 (1910): 15–60.

Sanders, Wilbur F. "Life of Governor Sidney Edgerton." *Rocky Mountain Magazine* 1 (1901): 437–53.

Stuart, Granville. "A Memoir of the Life of James Stuart." *Contributions to the Historical Society of Montana* 1 (1876): 36–79.

Webster, N. H. "Journal of N. H. Webster." *Contributions to the Historical Society of Montana* 3 (1900): 300–30.

Winner, Dorothy. "Rationing During the Montana Gold Rush." *Pacific Northwest Quarterly* 36 (1945): 115–20.

Index

Bannack, 31, 44; decided to spend winter in Bannack, 45

Edgerton, Pauline, born, 7; daughter of Sidney and Mary Wright Edgerton, 7, 9; member of Edgerton party, 11; photograph, 21; fell through ice and narrowly escaped drowning, 50; ill, 99, 123; letter to relatives and friends from, 115

Edgerton, Sidney, elected to Congress, 1, 5; appointed chief justice for Idaho Territory, 1, 7; governor of Montana Territory, 2; left Idaho Territory for Washington, D.C., 2, 55–56, 75, 75 fn.3; born, 4; graduated from law school, 4; interested in politics, 4; met Mary Wright, 4; parents, 4; schoolteacher, 4; children, 5, 7, 8, 9, 56, 86 fn.7, 135; delegate to convention that created Free-Soil party, 5; delegate to first Republican convention, 5; elected prosecuting attorney for Sumit County, Ohio, 5; married, 5; purchased Alpha Wright's farm, 5; defeated in election for Congress, 6; photograph, 6; member of Edgerton party, 11; photograph of Bannack home of, 40; purchased home in Bannack, 46, 63; description of home in Bannack, 46–47, 63–64, 119; furnishings in Bannack home, 47; guest of Henry Plummer, 49; never took oath as chief justice of Idaho Territory, 52; observed vigilante justice, 54; vigilantes secured howitzer from, 54, 74; agreed to go to Washington, D.C., to lobby for division of Idaho Territory, 55, 66; reportedly sanctioned vigilante movement, 55; appointed Montana's territorial governor, 56, 91; led Republican group in Montana Territory, 57; required legislators to take "Iron-Clad Oath of Allegiance" to the Union, 58, 105; financially supported Montana's first territorial legislature, 59; impatient with federal government's not appointing territorial secretary, 59–60, 101; fell in disfavor with Republican party, 60; left Montana with family, 60; resigned as Montana territorial governor, 60; returned to Washington, D.C., 60; investments in Montana profitable, 61, 61 fn.74; preparations for trip to Washington, D.C., 71; arrived in Ohio and departed for Washington, D.C., 81 fn.5; left Washington,

D.C., 86 fn.7; arrived in Bannack from Washington, D.C., 89–90; fishing expedition, 91; mining property, 94; called legislature to meet in Bannack, 99; Bannack citizens built office for, 102; performed duties of territorial secretary, 102, 103; gifts from lobbyists to, 103, 103 fn.16, 107, 109; vetoed legislative bill concerning testimony in cases of white and black men, 113, 113 fn.1; considered moving from Bannack, 114; dagarreotype taken of home, 120; legislature raised salary as governor, 120; no salary received from federal government, 120; planned to move to Virginia City, 122–23, 123 fn.6; attempted to raise volunteer militia to deal with hostile Indians, 125 fn.8; went into private law practice, 135; died, 135

Edgerton, Sidney (Jr.), born, 7; son of Sidney and Mary Wright Edgerton, 7, 9; member of Edgerton party, 11; near accident, 26; page for legislative house, 106 fn.18; wages as page, 108; birthday, 128

Edgerton, Volney, brother of Sidney Edgerton, 8, 133, 133 fn.11

Edgerton, Wright, born, 7; son of Sidney and Mary Wright Edgerton, 7, 9; member of Edgerton party, 11; ill, 66, 97, 99; considered for page for one of the legislative houses, 103; page for legislative council, 106, 106 fn.18; wages as page, 108; worked in Bannack post office, 130, 133

F

Fenn, Richard, friend of the Edgertons. 8, 87 fn.8; built schoolhouse on Yankee Flat in Bannack, 51; finished cabin, 95

Fisk, James, government expedition, 36

Fort Laramie, Edgerton party reached, 22

Freemasonry, in Bannack, Montana, 39–40

G

Gallatin Valley, Montana, 118, 118 fn.3

Geer, Almarette, member of Edgerton party, 7, 12

ized in Bannack, 54, 74–75; organized in Virginia City, 54, 73–74; secured howitzer from Sidney Edgerton, 54, 74; attitude of populace toward, 55; *see also* Outlaws

Virginia City, Montana, established, 44; capital of Montana Territory, 59; vigilantes formed and active in, 73–74; residents planned to build house for territorial governor, 123, 123 fn.6

W

Whitman, Nina, daughter of Sidney and Mary Edgerton, 3

Wright, Alpha, farmer, 4; father of Mary Edgerton, 3

Wright, Benjamin, brother of Mary Edgerton, 7, 23, 23 fn.19; traveled to California, 11

Wright, Clement, brother of Mary Edgerton, 8, 73, 73 fn.1

Wright, Lucy, sister-in-law of Mary Edgerton, 8

Wright, Lucy Foster, mother of Mary Edgerton, 3; letters from Mary Edgerton, 63–65, 88, 95–96, 100–1, 108–9, 110–12, 117–18, 121–22, 122–24, 130–31

Wright, Nellie, sister-in-law of Mary Edgerton, 9

Wright, William, brother of Mary Edgerton, 4; founded Oberlin College, 4

This book designed by
Bailey-Montague & Associates
has been set in Intertype Baskerville
by Donald M. Henriksen
printed on Mountie Text
by Publishers Press
and bound by
Mountain States Bindery

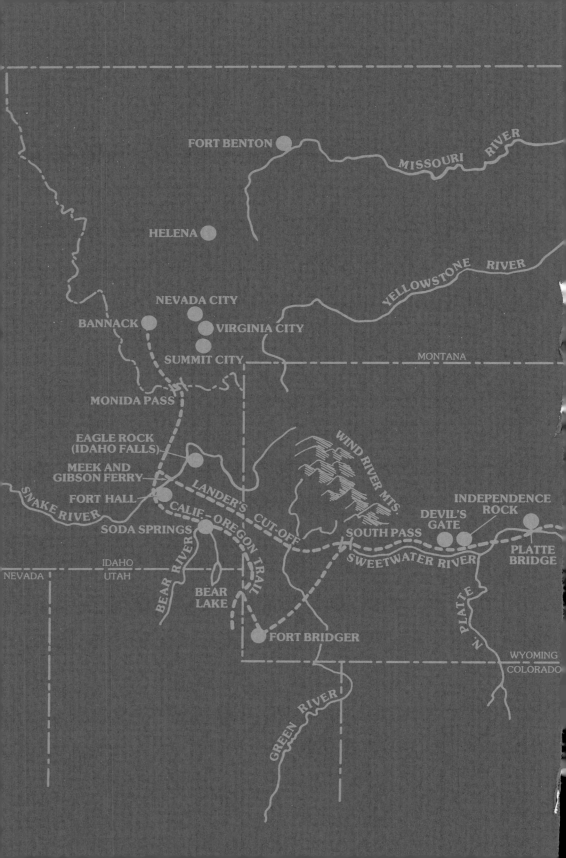